MW00610717

9 to 5 MILLIONAIRE

DON'T QUIT YOUR DAY JOB

PUBLICATIONS

JEMAL KING

PUBLICATIONS

Cover design: 120 Design Studio
Page design & layout: OA.Blueprints, LLC

Printed in the United States of America

ISBN: 978-1-942499-16-9

Contents

Dedication

To every nine to fiver with a millionaire
inside of them...

Acknowledgements

To My Parents

Mom, thank you for praying for me before I was born. Thank you for showing me what having unwavering faith really looks like. Thank you for teaching me that through Christ, all things are possible. I love you.

Dad, thank you for your continual sacrifice throughout the years so that we would be in a position to have better. Thank you for your protection and guidance into manhood. Thank you for being a perfect example of how a husband is supposed to love his wife and provide for his family. I love you.

Mom 2, when I was a young, ambitious teenager dating your youngest daughter, I'll never forget how you sowed into my life at a young age. You had me commit to memory Psalm 1:1-4, and it has guided me throughout my life. I love you.

Dad 2, thank you for trusting me as a man to take your daughter's hand in marriage. Now that I have two daughters, I can only imagine how scary that was seeing your youngest daughter get married. Thank you for accepting me as your) son.

To My Wife Camille

There are no words that I can write to sum up what you mean to me. Throughout most of my life, you've been right by my side. Over twenty-five years ago, we planned the life out that we now live. We wrote out the vision of how we wanted our life to be together. We sacrificed and worked hard together, and we prayed and held onto the vision together. Through it all, you never left my side! Remember the day we got married; the pastor told us that becoming one was a process that we would grow through. I can honestly say that we are now one! I love you more today than I did the day we said I do. Together there is nothing we can't do. Together forever. I love you!

To My Children

Ayanna, I'll never forget the feeling you gave me the first time I held you. You brought meaning to the word legacy in my life. You are the perfect teenager in our eyes, and we love that we can depend on you to be your very best. God has blessed you with a loving, caring, compassionate, hard-working spirit that will open doors for you that no one can shut! Continue to be you and never forget that, "With God all things are possible." - Matthew 19:26

Jasmine, the day you were born, I fell in love all over again. From early on in your life, there was nothing that you couldn't accomplish once you put your mind to it. God has blessed you with strength and wisdom, talent, and a loving heart. Always strive to be the best in everything you do and always remember Matthew 17:20 - "If you have faith as small as a mustard seed, you can say to this mountain, move from here to there, and it will move." Nothing will be impossible for you.

Jemal Jr., you are God's promise fulfilled in our life! Your mother and I prayed for seven years without ceasing for God to bless us with you. Your birth made my faith stronger. You are evidence that all things are possible to those who believe. God has blessed youwith the Spirit of Faith, love, and favor that will surpass all understanding. Never forget, 1 Samuel 1:27-28 - "I prayed for this child, and the Lord has granted me what I asked of Him; so now I give him to the Lord. For his whole life he will be given over to the Lord."

Vontrell, I will always remember how God saw the need to bring us together. I know you believe that I taught you so much over the years. However, I have learned from you as well. You taught me how to go through painful circumstances in life while persevering your way to the top and not making excuses. You taught me that a person's circumstances don't have to be their reality. You taught me how to love and raise another man's son as my own—and I thank you. We are so proud of the man you have become, and I am sure your heavenly parents are smiling down on you right now. Continue to keep God first in all that you do. Remember Psalm 37:23 - "The steps of a good man are ordered by the Lord, and he delighteth in his way."

To My Siblings
Karla, Tommie and Christy, if I could choose my siblings, I would still choose each of you. I wouldn't trade my siblings for the world. Each one of you holds a special part of my heart.

Without your love, protection, dedication, and support, this journey of mine would have certainly been less fulfilling. Thank you for adding so much value and love to my life. I love you.

My bonus sisters and brothers: Ted, Nekia, Ebony, Devanne, Coleman, and Desmond - thank you for supporting me and loving me as a brother. Our friendship and the memories that we share are invaluable. Thank you for being examples for all of our children.

Nieces and Nephews

Brittany, Kamron, Desmond Jr., Matthew, Caitlynn, Kayla, Jeremiah, Elijah, Ava, and Alyssa - success is in your DNA. I believe that great things are in your future, and I'm excited to witness God's blessings in each of your lives.

The Family

To Grandma Lila, Great-Aunt Dorothy, Great-Aunt Mattie, aunts, uncles, and cousins, my foundation is strong because of your influence, support, and love. I love each of you.

The Village

The Tolberts, The V. Darlings, The Cobbs, The Troopes, The Stewarts, The L. Darlings, The Sanfords, The Quinneys, The Hatchs, Dr. Alexis and family, The Browns, The Tramells, Tony Brown, Uncle Keith, B-Bad Butler, West, James and my god-daughter Legacy Amore.

Make Real Real Estate Real

To all of the Make Real Estate Real students and

the Alumni group. The invaluable and incomparable MRER Dream Team: April Troope, Damon Stewart, Perdure "Coach" Carter, Nathan Majors, Mark Buford, AEM Acquisitions (Aaron, Evan, Mike) Natasha Robinson, Terri Couser, Darrell Mitchell, Adrian Zeno, and Natalie Peralta. The best is yet to come. Thank you for rocking with me. Let's go!!

ETA Squad
Eric Thomas, Dede, CJ, Karl, Josh, Ashante Tucker, Nicky, Jose, Isaiah, Nicky, Dave Benson, Marshall Fox, Tiffany Haynes, VaLarie H., Inky Johnson, Tiphani Montgomery, Shawn Stevenson, LaShanna, Moose, Charles Terry, TJ, Tobe Nwigwe, Chuck, Wedzere and Morgan Naval, Valerie H., Kam Quinney, Ken Nelson, Quest and Faith Green, Josh Letsis, Dr. Downs, Anthony Flynn, Willie Mo Jr., David Shands, Maja Sly, Val, Kendall Flicklin, Kantis, ETA Game Changers, ETA Masters of The Game, Kiah Chism, Jamie Cook, Jeremy Anderson and all volunteers and supporters of ETA. Thank you for welcoming me into the family!

Spiritual Leaders
Reverend L.K. Curry, Apostle Joseph L. Stanford, Apostle Nathaniel Dodd (Uncle Jr), and Pastor John F. Hannah. Thank you for pouring into me. Your influence, your words, and examples have helped guide me spiritually along my journey.

Groups/Organizations
Bogan Bengals High School Football Team, Western Illinois University Leathernecks Foot-

ball Team, Omega Psi Phi Inc. and my brothers of Gangsta EB, Chicago Police Department (006 District and Headquarters), TADD Realty, Lakewood University, CHAMPS Male Mentoring Program, Renovo Financial, King's Kiddie Kingdom and Illinois Security Professionals.

In Loving Memory
Grandma Lorean, Grandma Rena, Grandma Dodd, Papa Shelly, Grandpa Charlie, Uncle Lester, Uncle James and Lil Tommie. I miss your presence on this earth, but I will never forget the memories and life lessons. I'll always treasure the special meals, valuable advice, and workouts, as well as the laughter and love. I will continue to work hard to bring honor to your legacy. I love you.

To My GOD
Heavenly Father, I thank you and honor you for Always ordering my steps in life and allowing me to tap into the power that works in all of us!

"Live life on the left side of the menu."

JEMAL KING

Introduction

The Backbone of America

At the time that I'm writing this book, the world is battling a pandemic. Over twenty million people in the United States alone have already filed for unemployment due to company layoffs, the President has cut funding for the World Health Organization, and the very people that Congress said should be able to survive on only $7.25/hour are now keeping this country alive. The grocery store workers, the police, the hospital staff, the postal workers, to name a few. Daily, they're being forced to risk their lives to ensure that society has a sense of normalcy and access to the essentials. Or at least, they're trying to. On top of our economic and health systems toppling over, a global civil rights movement is brewing. It seems like we're hashtagging another Black body every day. The violence from police shootings and alt-right racists has reached a brink, and the very earth is protesting against it. In the last few months we've had Black women get shot to death in their sleep, Black men shot in the back for deescalating a fight, Black bodies being found lynched across the U.S., and of course; the notorious knee to the neck that's happened at least twice since George Floyd's murder. You would think that we'd all understand Black Lives Matter isn't a trend or a superiority complex. The movement has never pushed for us to be deemed greater and more important than any other racial

9 to 5 Millionaire

group. It's simply demanding that we receive fair treatment because all lives will never matter until Black ones do too. As a retired officer, I recognize I hold a special take on all of this. I understand the dangers of the job and the risk that's associated with wearing the badge. The nervousness of potentially never returning home because of the ill-fated choice of someone else. How stressful it is to think of another man telling your wife that you were killed. At the same time, I know that I wear something everyday that's seen as a target and I can't take it off; my skin. The fear of having dark skin has, and will, continue to trump the fears associated with being a cop. Black men and women face that same kind of stress every time they watch each other leave home, especially their children. Even with my badge, I had to face work-related issues that civilians wouldn't have to encounter. Without it, even with the resources that come with acquiring wealth, I'm just as nervous and cautious as any other Black person. What pains me the most is knowing that the working and impoverished classes are hit by these realities the most.

Yet, blue-collar workers are still doing what blue-collar workers do best. They're remaining loyal during the pressures of life, they're showing up at their best, and they're fighting to make sure their families aren't in need during one of the scariest pandemics (COVID-19 and systemic racism) we've seen in nearly a century. In other words, they're not throwing their hands up in defeat.

They're throwing their hands up for battle. But of course, we aren't surprised by this. Blue-collar workers have been the backbone of this nation since being blue-collar was a thing. According to the Oxford Dictionary, blue-collar is defined as, "Relating to manual work or workers, particularly in an industry." These are the jobs that you and your neighbor take on like firefighting, custodial jobs, manufacturing and teaching. The jobs that make success stories like Jeff Bezos, Madam CJ Walker, and me—the 9 to 5 Millionaire— so heart-wrenching and inspiring.

I'm writing this because I wanted to let you know that I believe in the blue-collar family. I could say it took the police force, teachers, postal workers, and almost every other blue-collar job assisted in raising me. We carry some of the most sought after skill sets that employers covet. We're the ones who see smoke and run to put out the fire. We can put in long hours for the first shift and be back for the third. We take on responsibilities that our job titles don't even include. Mere floor workers step in as managers when the store needs supervision. We say yes to extra shifts when asked even though we want to attend our daughter's recitals or our son's tutoring session. When they preach to us about sacrifice, we already know what they're talking about. We're not lazy. We're just fed up, and understandably so. Any U.S. citizen can look around and realize the middle class no longer exists. In today's economy, you're either poor or rich. The poor are trading in time for money, working two or more jobs for real stability, settling for an okay paying job that takes your fire away. Meanwhile, the rich are trading in money for their time by investing in themselves and building a real legacy that they love. I would know because like I said earlier, I'm the 9 to 5 Millionaire. Blue-collar ethics built me for greatness. And it's because of my background that I hate to see the hardest working people suffering the most. Facing missed vacations, poor health conditions, even fighting the occasional eviction notice due to an unforeseen layoff. In a society where you're either poor or rich, we're forced to look at the major differences in lifestyle, access, and privilege. Now, let's be clear, this book isn't going to bash the wealthy. However, this book is going to call out the issues with society's heavyweight champs living like underdogs. And more importantly, teach them how they can keep their blue-collar jobs and build multi-million dollar companies at the same time.

Because the truth is this, you can be as wealthy as you decide. No one, not your boss, not your family, not Facebook, and not even your fears; get to dictate your income. Your job may provide a salary, but that doesn't mean that's all you're able to generate in a year. For example, if you're a teacher generating $50,000 a year, that only means your district is supplying you with $50,000; It's not that you're confined to only making that much money every 365 days. So if you decided that you wanted to make $250,000 that year instead, that's your decision to make. Now I know this might sound fanciful or even insulting to make you believe anything is possible. The truth is that I've done this one hundred times over. By the time I was twenty-six years old I was the wealthiest officer in my department, and it's not because of the minimal percentage raises that we'd get every so often. It's because I realized I could create more income on the side while also serving the city of Chicago.

The point of this book is to remind people that you can do both. How often do you log online just to be told that you have to leave your job to chase your dreams? Talk about total BS. That's such a crazy assumption to make about people! Everyone doesn't hate their jobs, and I'd even bet that most people don't even dislike their jobs. They just hate not being able to live the life of their dreams because of it. If people were able to clock-in, do their jobs, take their dream vacations, pay for their children's tuition and simply give more, there'd be far fewer job complaints. Because no matter how entrepreneurial we're becoming as a society, we need blue-collar jobs to keep the world aligned. Imagine if every teacher decided, "I'm done teaching! I'm going to go start my own company and only work for myself!" That'd be a sad day in education because we need teachers! Who's going to teach our children the importance of learning and reinforce it with skills such as writing, reading and critical thinking? Or if every firefighter said, "Putting out fires is a total waste of time, I'm going to start my own business." There'd be anarchy! Now I know you might feel this is a bit dramatic, even humorous, but it's the truth. People who tell you that you aren't serious enough about your life because you're still working your full-time job are manipulators! And to keep it real with you, they're more than likely trying to scam you into giving them your money.

So no, this book is not here to endorse "leave your day job" culture. Quite the contrary. It's here to emphasize the complete opposite. Keep your day job because building wealth is a numbers game! For example, remember the teacher making $50,000 a year from earlier? Let's turn the character into a teacher. Imagine if he decided to go and open a barbershop on the side and built systems that allowed him to generate an additional $100,000 a year. He's now generating (different than profiting) $150,000 a year! If he listened to these gurus, he'd believe that to make more money with the barbershop; he needs to quit being a teacher. And that is the exact opposite of how wealthy people move. That belief stands on the foundation of trading in more time as the only way of bringing in more cash. But think about what he can do with $150,000 versus quitting his day job and trying to survive and build a business from the profits of his $100,000? He'd be adding unnecessary weight on top of his vehicle to riches because he feels too pressured to stay in his gifting as a teacher by day.

What I want you to do is to erase everything that you've heard about entrepreneurship and wealth-building prior to this book. Read the remaining pages with a fresh and open mind, because you can be all in and still stay at your 9 to 5. Remember, building a legacy is a numbers game focused on revenue and your use of time.

At no point in this book am I going to tell you that the key to a better future is for you to start working harder. Being legacy-driven requires more efficiency and systems, not brute force. In other words, I'll be teaching you how to work smarter and not harder. If you already go that hard for a company that doesn't promise to take care of your children, I know you're capable of keeping that same energy for yourself. So again, remove everything you think is true about wealth and let's redefine it together.

By the time you're reading this, you'll more than likely already feel the shifts that are taking place in the world. Our new normal is setting in. The 1% are no longer the gatekeepers of riches (although it may feel like it sometimes). They're just hyper-aware of where we're headed in the world. And if people that have their great-grandchildren's riches secured have to be aware of what's going on, how much more aware should blue-collar workers be? Remember when I said that the middle class no longer exists? Well, that means only having one stream of income is too close to having zero! Your 9 to 5 was never meant for you to work just to be able to pay your liabilities (bills, insurance, etc). It's meant to be used as a tool that can allow you to purchase income-producing assets that pay for your liabilities! That's the game we're playing now! Between pandemics, government shutdowns, artificial intelligence replacing labor centered work, and more; job security just isn't secure. You're the only one that can prepare your home for the worst situations you can imagine. And one job can't handle that kind of responsibility alone. Let's make it practical. Although it's possible to raise children with only one person in the home, it's taxing, stressful and sometimes depressing. But when you have two healthy adults raising a family, you have a bit more harmony. And when you add in a village, those children are set up to be unstoppable and the parents get the breaks they need to be the loving and sound parents they want to be. It's the same way with our income. One stream can handle the basics, two streams can create some harmony, but three-plus can create bliss and security.

And the best way to be able to build these streams is to learn how to become a character in your life story. Look, you're already multi-faceted. You're the home chef that's a car salesman by day. You're a custodian that paints with oil colors at night. Or the officer that's known for having the best home garden in the neighborhood. You have to start seeing how expansive you really are! You're not just your 9 to 5 title. You're a human being and that means you're destined for greatness. All of those gifts and skills laying dormant inside of you are just waiting on you to say yes! So get your notepad out and be ready to take notes, because we're starting your journey to wealth - *now!*

JEMAL KING

VISION

Chapter 1

COPS & ROBBERS

Growing up, my entire world was blue-collar. Here's the scene:

Our entire neighborhood lived in what we called Georgian style-homes. The outside was a dark-red brick accented with white panels, concrete steps that lead to the front door, old-English shutters to block the sun on the window panels, and the roofs always made a triangular peak middle. Inside, there were three bedrooms upstairs. You had a smaller bedroom, a mid-size, and a larger bedroom. My parents occupied what we call the master bedroom, my sisters were in the medium-sized room, and my brother and I shared the smallest room. When my oldest sister moved out, my brother and I moved to the mid-size room, and baby girl got her own space in the smaller bedroom.

In the entire house, there was only one full-sized bathroom on the second floor (imagine the routine we used to have to maintain for six people with one full-sized bath). When you first walked into the house, you immediately saw our living room, dining room, and then the kitchen. We lived in about twelve hundred square feet, plus a basement because we stayed in the Midwest. The goal was to add another bathroom downstairs after saving up from your part-time job; that's how we decked out our homes.

There were always groups of children playing games outside with one another, making sure not to bump any of the cars parked in front. There would be older kids playing a pick-up game of basketball at any point in the day, girls jumping double dutch, and everyone playing tag. However, we knew we had to be back inside before the street lights turned on; this was the universal sign of playtime being over." But before the lights came on, we made sure we got in our rap battles. It wasn't uncommon to see someone walking down the street with their Sony radio on their shoulder, blasting out beats for the neighborhood kids to rap to. You'd hear everyone from Run DMC to LL Cool J rapping out of some teenager's speakers, while the adults were barbecuing on the side of their homes. We lived in the kind of neighborhood where everyone knew they were welcome to come and get a plate. Afterward, the adults would sit down to discuss what I like to call "The Blue-Collar Blues" while listening to Motown's magical sounds.

You might wonder, "Why is Jemal telling us about his neighborhood?" I'm sharing with you the details of my neighborhood and my family throughout this book because I'm a firm believer in context. It's the weight of knowing your teacher as a human and not just some guru that allows you to take their lessons and go and apply them. My goal is to share the pieces of my life as a testament for you to see yourself and say, "Well, if Mal came from that and became a multi-millionaire, then I can be a multi-millionaire too." That's why

I'm starting this book off by talking to you about the cops and robbers that make up my family. You see, my lineage is the epitome of the working class.

My father Tommie, aka Superman, was born in Mississippi, and he's the third of thirteen children. His family migrated to the Midwest when he was just a boy. So at his core, he's a southern man raised by the inner city. He taught us so much about manhood that has shaped me into the husband and father I am today. He worked hard to provide for his family, but he was always present to teach us valuable lessons about life and work ethic, relationships and making it in life. My mother Rosie, was born and raised on the West Side of Chicago. She epitomizes grace and beauty and is the ultimate definition of a woman, wife and mother. She's the perfect role model of faithfulness, as we witnessed her serving on various boards in our church.

Just like any top-rated romance movie, my parents met in either kindergarten or first grade (that's their biggest argument). Eventually, my father would join the military; they'd marry and give birth to my first two siblings Karla and Tommie. After some time, they'd eventually give birth to two more children. Our parents taught us so much about being happily married for over fifty years.

Growing up, I've always known my father as an officer for the Chicago Police Department. He loved his work, respected his title, and handled the controversy of being a Black man with a government job with grace. I never witnessed him abuse his power in our home, nor did he make a habit of complaining about the nature of his career. My father was and is a man's man. He went to work every day and made sure he was the father we needed him to be when he was home. Even without a father in his life, he was able to step-up and raise four children and take care of his loving wife. My father was such an amazing man that it came to no surprise when the first Black Mayor of Chicago promoted him to sergeant. By the time my father got promoted, it was the 1980s and his advancement in rank, by becoming what we refer to as a White Shirt at the force, was the pinnacle of building a legacy.

Meanwhile, my mother was so involved with us that she'd frequently show up to my school to volunteer and help different teachers out. She showed up so much I thought she was working there too at the time. Her schedule would include being a crossing guard for the neighborhood kids in the morning and showing up later in the afternoon to serve again. After a while, she would begin working for the sheriff's department, too, which meant zero games were played in our homes when it came to discipline and education. And the same energy she had surrounding these two pillars was the same energy she kept with religion. I can't remember a time my mother didn't have us in the church house on Sunday morning, whether my father had to work or not.

Those are my parents; two service-driven people who spent their entire careers being blue-collar and supporting fellow blue-collar workers. They worked hard to make sure my siblings and I had what we needed in life regarding food, shelter, safety, and community. So much so, all of my friends that I was allowed to visit came from families of officers too. Here's the structure of the neighborhood I grew up in.

Out of fifty homes, fifteen of them were occupied by officers. That means someone on my father's force owned every third house in our neighborhood. The other homes were occupied by other blue-collar families like mail carriers, teachers, and factory workers. Everyone in the community had between three to four kids, worked from 9 am to 5 pm, held a potential weekend part-time job, hosted Sunday cookouts, drove the same cars, and even our houses looked alike. By the time I was six years old, I was familiar with terms like furlough, pension, union, 401k, FMLA, aka sick leave and contract. All of the people in my life lived, breathed, and preached blue-collar traditions, customs, and beliefs. They especially understood that the more rank you could acquire via titles and certificates led to better pay and lifestyle options.

THE BLUE-COLLAR GLOSSARY

Furlough: leave of absence, especially that granted to a member of the armed services. It's also a paid-vacation time for the working class.

Pension: a regular payment made during a person's retirement from an investment fund to which that person or their employer has contributed during their working life.

Union: an organized association of workers formed to protect and further their rights and interests, a labor union.

401k: the tax-qualified, defined-contribution pension account defined in subsection 401(k) of the Internal Revenue Code.

Medical leave aka sick leave: the number of days per year for which an employer agrees to pay employees who are sick.

Contract: a written or spoken agreement, especially one concerning employment, sales, or tenancy, intended to be enforceable by law.

Deferred compensation: an arrangement in which a portion of an employee's income is paid out at a later date after which the income was earned, usually for thirty years.

Credit Union: a nonprofit-making money cooperative whose members can borrow from pooled deposits at low-interest rates.

Tax Return: a form on which a taxpayer makes an annual statement of income and personal circumstances, used by the tax authorities to assess tax liability.

Retroactive pay or back pay: refers to income owed to an employee from a previous pay period. Retroactive pay may happen for several reasons, such as incorrect salary compensation or wages for hours worked, or a pay increase.

No call no show: an employee's absence from work without notifying the employer.

WORDS WE NEVER HEARD GROWING UP

941 Taxes: an IRS return that employers use to report their FICA taxes paid and owed for the period.

Bi-Coastal: living on, taking place in, or involving two coasts, especially the Atlantic and Pacific coasts of the U.S.

Dividends: a sum of money paid regularly (typically quarterly) by a company to its shareholders out of its profits (or reserves).

Passive income: earnings derived from a rental property, limited partnership, or another enterprise in which a person is not actively involved.

Limited liability company: a corporate structure in the United States whereby the owners are not personally liable for the company's debts or liabilities. Limited liability companies are hybrid entities that combine the characteristics of a corporation with those of a partnership or sole proprietorship.

Generational wealth: an aspect of financial planning that is geared toward passing down stable, significant financial resources to future generations.

Sabbatical: a period of paid leave granted to a worker for study or travel, traditionally one year for every seven years worked. Or a period that's taken by someone self-employed to have a study-vacation.

Profit-Sharing: a system in which the people who work for a company receive a direct share of the profits.

Joint Ventures: a commercial enterprise undertaken jointly by two or more parties which otherwise retain their distinct identities.

Partnerships: a legal form of business operation between two or more individuals who share management and profits.

IRS: the Internal Revenue Service (IRS) is a bureau of the Department of Treasury tasked with the enforcement of income tax laws and oversees federal income taxes.

PNL: a profit and loss statement is a financial statement that summarizes the revenues, costs, and expenses incurred during a specified period, usually a fiscal quarter or year.

Being Defined By Your Benefits Package

Sameness is a massive part of being blue-collar too. My father frequently told us that we could do whatever we wanted to do in life, even despite the obstacles that we'd face for the color of our skin or our socioeconomic status. Even still, the sameness was so prominent that even words like the above felt like we were still set-up to just be good citizens, marry well, get a good house, and raise good kids. It would seem as if the entire neighborhood was training their generations just to play defense with life.

But like any other family, I had relatives playing offense for the wrong team. In particular, my family is from the West Side of Chicago, before moving to the South Side, and there was plenty of mess for my family to find themselves in if they weren't working city jobs. Even one of my favorite uncles stayed in and out of jail because of his decisions. However, he changed his life around and began to work with me on projects and to this day we have a great relationship. When drugs started to slowly find its way into our neighborhood, people got stuck between two worlds. Being a worker of the city or pushing the city's illegal products. It's crazy how important it is to have access to people that believe in you and support you. It's so easy to find yourself living a fast-life guaranteed to take you to a judge's courtroom or the morgue.

So on one side of my world, there was the police

force. My father, the sergeant. His older brother, the chief of police. His other brother was a sheriff at Cook County jail, and another brother was a military police officer. Then, there were the robbers, the pushers, and the bangers. And if you ask me, it was a representation of the times.

See, in 1968, Martin Luther King Jr. was assassinated, setting the tone for the seventies . By 1972 the Watergate scandal was brewing, and Shirley Chisolm was campaigning to become the first black woman to try and become the president of the United States. The hippie movement was starting up; all while feminists were pushing for equal rights in the workplace. In 1974, not only did we experience the impeachment of a U.S. President, but we also experienced the Oil Embargo Crisis, putting the country's energy supply at a critical condition for several months. Yet, the likes of Bill Gates were launching companies like Microsoft in 1975, plus; college and university enrollment went from 282,000 in 1966 for African-Americans to 1,062,000 by 1976! All of these changes were occurring before I was even on this earth. I was simply born into the aftermath of the fast-moving sixties and recovering seventies. And when the world is shifting on every scale imaginable, it impacts the livelihoods of the millions of people working day in and out to provide for their families. We finally started getting access to better raises and titles. For some of us, we were the first generation to receive access to having managerial positions, a college education and high-level positions. And still, there are so many issues that we have yet to recover from. One of the biggest detriments was corporations' hand in limiting the vision of the blue-collar family.

Every time I have the privilege of working with someone in a traditional job, I ask them what their vision is for their life. The conversation usually goes a little like this:

What do you see for yourself in life?

"Well, I want to get a good job, marry the right person, get a lovely house, and take care of our family. I don't need anything too fancy; I just want to be there for my loved ones and retire at some point."

And every time I hear different variations of those words, my heart is heavied. Here's why— nothing about the statement above is a representation of a clear vision. Comments like those represent a desire to survive the very opposite of thriving! Of course, we should all want to be able to do right by our loved ones. Of course, we should desire an abode that we feel safe in. But those are the bare basics of living! The American dream for the working class and the rich are two very different definitions and standards. And it's because our visions are typically not even our own.

When we try to envision ourselves as the best version of ourselves, we can only see what we've experienced thus far. Our exposure levels are so limited by our customs that we don't think about having chefs and entire gyms inside our homes, or visiting a new country twice a year. When someone even mentions things as such, we call them frivolous, doing too much, or braggadocious. Why? Because when you got the position at your new job, they immediately talked to you about your 401k and your retirement plan. They want you to immediately buy into the idea of staying with them the next thirty to forty years of your life. They never asked you how you'd like to live while working for them. To be frank, it's not their job to do so. But that doesn't mean we can't start to create visions that go far beyond the 10% exposure to life's gems that we've witnessed.

Think about your current community. How many homes or apartments look the same? How many times have you been able to walk outside and see a car that's not manufactured by Ford, Toyota, Nissan or Chevrolet, on your street? When's the last time you balled out at the movie theatre without having to sneak snacks to save money? How often do you use up all of your vacation days every year? When's the last time you even took a mental health day? How about the last time your child's school took them overseas for a lesson on understanding cultural differences?

By the time you turned seventeen, the world had started demanding that you knew what you wanted to do in life, and made you think it was the same as knowing who you wanted to be. And for that, I'm sorry. It's not fair that you're expected to go into debt to figure out if we like something enough to do it for the rest of our lives. It's certainly not fair to have to settle for raises that come every five or so years with a minimal increase. But this is your time to start over. So I'm going to ask you to read the third part of this chapter while asking yourself this question: *What is my vision?*

The Preview of Your Life

Anytime someone asks me to define vision, I always go back to this comparison. Before you see a movie, the preview is the visible marketing tool that makes you decide whether you want to view it. It exists merely to grab your attention and to show you what's to come in the film. You get to see pieces of some of the best scenes in the project, and if it's constructed correctly, it gets your blood pumping, your heart racing, and excites you enough to say you want to spend your money on the show. It's a thirty-second clip to describe what the next two hours or more of your life will be like.

That's what a vision is.

Your vision is meant to include the crazy, larger than life, snippets of your dreams. It is literally one of the most important things to have in your life. As the proverb verse goes, *Where there is no vision, the people will perish* - Proverbs 29:18. I don't know about you, but I tend to take phrases like that seriously and literally. I've lost so many people because they couldn't answer what they truly wanted out of life. They had no vision, which meant they lacked direction. And a lack of leadership leads to a lifestyle of being thrown each and every way by the toss of life's hand. I might be one of the first people to ask you to even think about these things, and that's okay, but I need you to ask yourself, what hope for the future do you have currently? What is this hope placed on? I ask because whatever you envision for yourself is what allows you to remain hopeful for better days. With the drastic shifts that we're all currently enduring with this new normal, hope and vision will be the only things to keep you focused on better days. Days that you didn't just get through, but days that you were prosperous in! Now I know it's hard for your mind to think further than what you've already seen. For that reason, I want to share the story of my birth with you.

What Vision Does For You

I was born on both June 21 and the 22. Half my body arrived on the evening of the 21 at 11:58 pm, but I was entirely delivered by 12:01 am June 22. I like to joke that this is why I'm able to live in two worlds simultaneously by being the 9 to 5 Millionaire. But to be honest, I think this particular way of entering the world is a testament to me being the only child my parents had to pray for. They had my two older siblings while my father was in the military. Soon after Tommie's birth, they began to try and conceive me so I would be close in age to him. To their surprise, they experienced troubles getting pregnant. For context, this was the early seventies, so there was no In-vitro fertilization (IVF) treatment. The first IVF baby was born a year after I was. So you have two hard-working, God-fearing, amazing parents who suddenly couldn't conceive their third child without access to technology to help me get here. For them, it must've felt like being blindsided.

But instead of giving up on me, they continued to try for nearly five years. Five years. Imagine what the outside world was saying to them? I can imagine it's some of the same things they told my wife and I about my son.

"Why don't you two just give up?"

"You already have two beautiful children."

"You two are still trying?"

"It's okay if you don't get pregnant again. Some women can't even have one child. Be grateful."

"You already have one daughter and one son, why do you need more?"

Despite what the world was saying around them, they had a vision for their home, and they knew it included more children. That's the power of having a vision! You don't put a timeline on what's to come; you just keep trying until it meets you! And they were so blessed by their faith; they even conceived my baby sister after me. The process of them continuing to create a life while one piece of their dream was still manifesting itself; shows commitment to a bigger vision than themselves. And clearly, I'm grateful they didn't give up on me during year two or after they crossed year four. Because had they stopped, I'd never be able to impact the lives I'm blessed to serve. I wouldn't have my own legacy to care for. I wouldn't have had the opportunity to give back to them for their commitment. And any time you slow up, or you stop before you reach the real vision you have for yourself, you not only miss out on the vision itself, but you miss out on the perks that come with it. Remember, the vision is just a preview of your life to come. There are so many other beautiful things that will happen in your fulfilling it, blessings you didn't even dream up. The entire year of 1977 was a huge transition period for my family. My father was accepted into the Chicago Police Department that year and my parents moved from the West Side of Chicago to the South Side and bought a new house. It was a year of fruitful expansion for them, all because they were faith-filled and vision-led people.

This story is an example of the difference between having a vision and having sight. Vision makes you lift yourself out of your current reality to see what could happen ten years down. Sight looks at what's exactly in front of it and says, *"That's the next step.* You don't need faith to look in front of you. But vision not only sees point B, it can also dream up points C through Z. That's what the next two chapters are going to teach you to do because you don't have time to keep settling! You don't have the privilege of saying, "I'm going to continue to accept what I've been given." We're here to live our lives! To force us to grow and expand and learn! Our blue-collar background says that we can wait until we re-tire...that we should give our companies our best thirty years (if we're lucky enough to only work for thirty years) while they take care of us for our worst fifteen. Even though we know we won't be taken care of how retirees were taken care of in the nineties. Pensions no longer exist. Loyalty to skill and tenure doesn't exist. There isn't enough money in social security to give you the lavish retirement you've been sold. But let's say you go the route you've been taught. You'll more than likely never receive the things you work for thirty years to get because life happens. You get old and tired, or you get sick and die, and you never live the dream your thirty-year-old-self created.

And that's no way to live a life.

Chapter 2

MILLION DOLLAR ASPIRATIONS

One of the harsh realities when it comes to understanding vision is the unlearning that comes with it. Most of the time, people dream entirely too small. The base of their dreams into their current surroundings, experiences, exposure, and many other factors. But if you look up the definition of a dream, it means a cherished aspiration, ambition, or ideal, according to the Oxford Dictionary. Do you know what it means to cherish something? Again, according to Oxford, it means to protect or care for lovingly. Think about all the things you love in your personal life. It could be your children, your freedom, your health, whatever. But when's the last time you cherished your aspirations, ambitions, and ideals? This very definition lets us know that dreaming is about going above and beyond the norm, so much so that you're willing to protect it and care for it along the way.

This is how I know most working-class people aren't dreaming yet. Dreams invoke a deep connection based on the feelings that they manifest while you're creating it. You should be able to feel your dream, smell it even. It should be so bright that you're ready to identify every single piece of it. That way, you can use it as motivation during trying times. I think most people are only thinking about their futures and labeling it a dream. Why? Because if I were to ask you what your dream was, you'd probably tell me something that you can already see manifesting in your life. You'd be using your sight, not your vision. Here's an example of just thinking of what's next in your life:

Let's say you're a police officer, and I ask you what your dreams are. Using your sight would have you answer the question by saying you dream of being promoted to sergeant. This might sound like it's an excellent way to answer my question, but the truth is, that's not a dream at all. Being promoted to sergeant after being a police officer is the literal next step. All you did was think of what's next in your life and called it a dream. Remember when we compared using your sight to being able to see point B after point A, but your vision is seeing all the way to point Z? Well, that's the same thing here. Do you know what a dream would look like if you were a police officer? Saying you wanted to become the Mayor of Police— now that's being able to see point Z!

This idea of being able to dream big and have unimaginable visions for yourself goes into asking yourself whether your dreams sound crazy to you based on everything currently around you. See, an idea should be so mad that it requires a lifestyle shift. When they're not, you're not forced to make any changes to your daily life. So you'll continue to go day to day living the same way because you don't have any compass guiding you towards what your life needs to start looking like. The other side of dreaming crazy is that it sets up boundaries for your accomplishments. Along the way to creating the vision you have for yourself, you'll begin to experience several life wins. Having a dream that's larger than yourself is to ensure that you don't get comfortable at any of these levels. As humans, we're wired to stop wherever we set the finish line. Take sprinters, for example. Track coaches emphasize running through the line because you'll get the best outcome by pushing beyond what everyone else considers the finish.

Another example is to think about professional football. If a collegiate-athlete only dreams about making it to the league, they'll be satisfied upon being drafted. Everything that happens afterward will simply be a consequence of his initial dream. On the flip side, if a collegiate athlete dreams of making it to the NFL Hall of Fame, he'll be forced to excel at every stage of his career. The one that aspires to be a hall of famer won't slow down after winning a couple of Super Bowls. They'll be mini-accomplishments compared to his long-term vision. When people ask me why I never slowed down after I hit my first million, I use it as a teaching pillar. I never said I just wanted to be a millionaire. I said I wanted to be a multi-millionaire!

This type of dreaming requires a level of audacity about yourself. A lot of people are going to try and stop you with statements like:

"Who does (s)he think they are?"

"So you think you're better than what we're do-ing?"

"Are you not grateful for the life you already have?"

"People are worried about their next meal, and you're thinking about being a millionaire. Sounds selfish to me."

The significant part about a vision though, is that it's personal, and there's no such thing as over-dreaming! It doesn't matter if it doesn't make sense to anybody else as long as it aligns with your heart! Besides, over-dreaming would be an oxymoron. The entire point is to go above and beyond! It's about being and having anything that you can visualize. There are no limitations on dreams. In reality, you might have flaws, but the goal will inspire you enough to get beyond these. Now I'm not saying to make them a real-ity; all you need to do is think about something bigger than yourself. Faith without work is what? Dead, that's what. But the dream is the fuel to the vehicle that'll get you to your final destination.

One of the reasons we struggle so hard with this concept is because of our current educational system. I'm not knocking college at all, but the fact that we require seventeen-year-olds to de-cide what they want to be for the rest of their lives is ludicrous. The first question you get asked in college is, "What do you want to major in at school?" There's nothing fair about it. You barely even know what you like about yourself at the age of seventeen, let alone if you like a field enough to want to do it for the next thirty years. Lucky for you, you get to start over. Yep. It doesn't matter how old you are at the time you're reading these words. You have my permission and the freedom to make a change! So just like they asked you to choose a major at the age of seventeen, I'm asking you to pick a dream, not only a degree. What do you want? Do you know what you want to major in life? It's okay to make a pivot!

I keep hammering this idea of knowing what you want because we're creatures of habit. If you knew what you wanted, you'd go after it until you finally had it. The only difference between the wealthy and you is that they know what they want. So if you can clearly articulate what your dream is, you can start creating a concrete plan. I'm a massive fan of reverse engineering, my success. When we know exactly where we want to be in each area of our life, where we want to be in five years, ten years, twenty years, we can engineer the life we want.

MILLIONAIRE MOMENTS

Anytime you see this pop-up in the book it means I want you to pause and take a "Millionaire Moment" to think. Today's moment to focus on is this:

When you think about your current lifestyle, how much of it did you intentionally or unintentionally manifest yourself? Think about the words you've used to describe yourself, the dreams you've had, and the things you've settled for up until today.

After taking a moment to reflect, feel free to write down your answer somewhere safe and you can even share it with me by sending me a message on Instagram: @9to5millionaire.

We've All Wanted More

So here's the story of when I first declared that I wanted to be a millionaire. My father would ask my siblings and me what we wanted to be when we grew up as a custom. On this particular day it went a little like this:

Pops: Alright, y'all, what do you want to be when you grow up?

Karla: I want to be a teacher!

Pops: That's great, Karla! Education is essential,

and we need teachers. Okay, what about you, Junior?

Tommie: I'm going to be a police officer just like you dad!

Pops: I'm honored, son! You know serving as an officer is in your blood. Now, how about you, Jemal? What do you want to be when you grow up?

Now it was my turn to answer but my little sister Christy who was 4 years old interrupted me and wanted to answer, so my dad asked her the same question.

Pops: What do you want to be when you grow up baby girl?

Christy: I wanna be a teacher just like my big sister!

Pops: That's great sweetie, the world needs more teachers!!

Pops: Okay son, your older sister wants to be a teacher, your big brother wants to be a cop like me and even your little sister wants to be an educator like Karla! So now, what do you want to be when you grow up?

At that very moment it felt like a huge spotlight was on me and everyone was staring. After taking the time to consider my thoughts carefully I took a deep breath and yelled out...

Me: I WANT TO BE A MILLIONAIRE!!!

My father's face slowly begins to shift into a look of curiosity and wonder

Pops: Okay son, millionaire? That's great, but what are you going to do to become a millionaire?

This was the first time In my life that I had to think about what vehicle I would use to get me to my million-dollar destination. Now at this age, I didn't actually know what job could make me a millionaire, but I remembered watching the likes of NFL football players like "Prime Time" Deion Sanders and "Bo Knows" Jackson who were millionaires by playing professional sports so I said...

Me: I'll play football.

Pops: I'll support whatever you do as long as you're the best at what you're doing.

At eight-years-old, I knew that being a millionaire was a part of my destiny. I wanted to be a millionaire and drive a Lamborghini, a car I never would've seen in my community. Looking back, I know my answer threw my father for a loop. Millionaire isn't exactly a term that you hear blue-collar babies using to label their future-selves. But how could you blame me? At eight, I watched shows like Lifestyles Of The Rich and Famous, the equivalent of MTV Cribs for the millennials reading this. The show was hosted by Robin Leach (for the majority of the seasons). It was an inside look into the worlds of what we would've considered the filthy rich. Now, we had one TV in our house so I would have to make sure that I was using my TV time to watch the show. I know I was drawn to it for two reasons. First, it was the first time I was introduced to get-whatever you-want culture. They'd be going to malls, events, and amusement parks, buying everything their eyes landed on. I'd never experienced anything like that before! Of course, we didn't grow up poor. Remember, both my parents worked, and we were middle class. But when we went to the amusement park, we brought our food with us. There was no buying each of the kids their large fountain drinks inside the collector's cups; we didn't eat lunch inside the park. Do you know what we did? When it was time for food breaks, we'd walk back to the car to sit down and eat our pre-packed turkey sand-wiches (now hot from the heat of the car), with a side of chips, and water to wash it all down. The money we spent at the park was designated to enjoying the actual rides, not the amenities. Shoot, even when it came to going to the movies. I remember my father telling us to lay down in the back of the truck as we pulled up to the drive-in theatre. I didn't understand why, but now I real-ize it was a way to save money. So you take my very middle-class experiences as a kid and put a TV show like Lifestyles of The Rich and Famous in front of me, and it was like an awakening to an entirely different world. That, coupled with see-ing the commercials of celebrities and athletes and seeing the lifestyles they were showcasing, all motivated me to want to be a millionaire be-fore I even knew fourth-grade math.

The second reason why I loved the show so much was because all of the homes and lifestyles looked different. My entire world was the same. I walked outside just to see the same framework on each home. I woke up and put on the same white shirt, black pants, and black belt as my older brother Tommie. We even had the same haircut and would pose the same in photos despite being four years apart! Even when I talk with one of my close friends and business associates CJ from (ETA), we pretty much lived the same life despite being four years apart and being raised in two completely different states. The Blue-Collar Way promotes sameness because of a lack of income limit options. So I knew that if I wanted to have different, I would have to do different. I would have to become a millionaire, and there wasn't a single blue-collar job that could get me there by itself.

Becoming The Stand-Out Kid

I'm not all that different now than I was as a child. Being and doing different things has always been a driving force for my decisions, actions and thoughts. If you would've asked one of my siblings to describe little Jemal, they might even say that I was bad. I was a boy's boy just like I'm a man's man - like my father. I intentionally would choose to do the opposite of my siblings just to stand out. My siblings kind of always agreed, even if all of them didn't like something. If the group said, "Hey, this is what we're going to do..." then they would all agree, and I would always just choose to be different and say no. I was (am) super opinionated, and I always used to try to find ways to disagree with someone. Defensive and bold would be the perfect words to describe the younger Jemal. But even to this day, I'll never back down from a challenge. I just didn't want to say and do what everybody else did. I hate being the same as everybody; honestly, it bothers me to this day.

Back then, though, they especially thought I was terrible because I would get into fights at school. The calls my parents would receive made it sound like adolescent Jemal was just rebelling again and bullying the other students. What the calls never disclosed was that I was fighting to protect my family name. See, although we lived in a neighborhood with a Black majority, my parents sent me to a mainly White elementary school. My parents realized that we were flooded with black culture in our community. They also understood that the world was not all black. This school would expose us to different cultures and languages. However, this new school environment also came with its own negative drawbacks. I had to fight in school because of these drawbacks. Like many other Black students in mostly White schools, I was called nigger so often it felt like my nickname. By the time I was old enough to understand the term's weightiness, I had fought to show I wasn't going to take being mocked. I'll never forget when they made a chant whenever I'd get into another fight. They would put me in a circle and throw another White kid in there, and they would chant this song:

"A fight, a fight,
A nigger and a White.
A fight, a fight,
A nigger and a White."

And the times when I would check my desk, and there'd be a note left for me that would say, "Go back to Africa nigger." So as you can see, I had quite a few reasons to be as bold as possible. But instead of letting it deter me from showing up well at school, I chose to make their ignorance fuel me to be better than everyone else. I competed in everything. I had to be the fastest at the school. My grades were pretty shaky, but when I realized I was fighting for something, something I couldn't even articulate back then, I also got those together. It didn't matter if it was a test, a quiz, a presentation, a gym class exercise, whatever; I wanted to show them that I could beat them even though they thought so little of me. Before you knew it, I went from being the nigger they'd throw into random fights to being class president by the time we were in the eighth grade and voted most popular and likely to succeed. Being in an environment like this taught me how to be comfortable with being the only one no matter what the only one stood for.

Circumstances like this can make anyone bolder than they were before. But to be honest, I think a lot of my boldness also came from my father. I didn't think he was Superman for nothing. The entire neighborhood would go to him for advice and personal matters like he was the town's wise man. But whenever he needed to transform from Clark Kent to Superman, he'd do it with ease. The story that's always stuck with me was when he beat up a group of drug dealers while he was off-duty (Keep in mind, officers are never indeed off of work). It was a day both him and my mother had off during the week, and they pulled up at our house during the day. As they stepped outside the car, a drug dealer at the house next door had the nerve to call my mother the equivalent of a female dog. My father was already on edge because the drugs were slowly making their way into our community, and they ironically enough landed themselves in the house next door. When he heard this young man curse my mother, it was the ultimate sign of disrespect. He ran inside the drug house, and a fight ensued. My mother called a 10-1, which is the code officers use to alert all other officers to stop what they're doing and assist a cop in need. After putting a whooping on a couple of them and getting some back-up, they shut down the drug house. As you see, fear wasn't a characteristic I inherited. My parents made bold decisions, worked risky careers, and raised four children well. You couple their influence with my personal experiences, I was set for becoming a stand-out kid.

The truth is, we're all meant to be stand-out kids. Sadly, some of us have experiences that stopped us from tapping into the difference that enables us to stand up for ourselves and shape our own thinking. My being called a nigger at school was fire for me, but it could have very well made another Black child give up hope (and that would've made perfect sense). But now that we're adults, if we truly want to shape futures that look different from what we've experienced, we have to learn how to start reshaping our realities by understanding the pieces of ourselves contrary to everyone else.

Don't Let Your Memories Shape Your Dreams

Everything I shared with you above could've been used as water to douse the flame under my hopes and aspirations. And for the majority of people, that's what they allow their memories to do. Most people aren't able to separate past occurrences from future possibilities. Because people usually don't know what they want in life, they go back to their memories and list things that they needed back then as their future dreams. For example, if I were to ask someone who grew up in a home where their next meal wasn't guaranteed, one of their goals growing up would be to be able to eat what they wanted when they wanted to. Although a fundamental human right, it's a dream to them because, at one point, it was a need. The issue is, that doesn't include a want. So when they reach an income level that allows them to get the groceries that they need from the store, they'll be satisfied due to their dreams' limitations. I'm trying to get you to see that a dream is outside the confines of your memories and inside the limitless possibilities of your imagination. If you're experiencing fear in your life, it's likely because you don't know what will happen in your future.

My memory says that I should be a bitter man, scarred from the disgusting reality of racism, settling for checks that I pick-up in a wooden box labeled alphabetically on the first and the sixteenth. My memory says that I should've dreamt of a world of Georgian styled homes and sneaking in my kids to the drive-in theatre to avoid paying for their tickets. But allowing myself to think outside my mental box has allowed me to dream dreams my ancestors couldn't have imagined. I'm a firm believer that the "...exceedingly, abundantly, above all that we ask or think..." - Ephesians 3:20 starts with taking down your dream blockers.

This means you have got to start training yourself to be able to look into the future. Not a simple three to five years either, but to begin visualizing what lifestyle you will be living in the next ten to twenty years. When it's time for you to breathe your last breath, what kind of access to resources will you have by then? How strong will your family legacy be? What kind of home will you be sleeping in? What countries did you visit before your passing? ? Please note that you have to remember to account for failure while you're thinking about your dreams. If not, you'll be like the rest of the world and give up when the going gets tough. Dreaming is mental work, but taking action is the sauce. You can't put a time limit on your dreams. That might sound contrary to the questions I asked you earlier, so let's break it down. Saying you want to accomplish a level of success within ten years doesn't mean you get to year ten and give up if it didn't pan out the way you hoped. The ten years is a compass, just like your dream, but there are always other factors that will either speed up or slow down our progress in life. And if your dreams feel like they're being delayed, maybe you're the one that's not ready for the dream. There's a process between dreaming and making a dream come true. The process is just as necessary as the actual dream itself. As blue-collar workers, I always wondered why it is so easy for us to see the end goal with our jobs via retirement, but we can't see it for our own lives and visions? When it comes to personal growth, we break at the mere thought of failure when we go to the ends of the earth to give a company all we have.

At some point, you've got to start to hate losing. You've got to get fed up with being told how to live your life. You have to hate it to the point where you're like, "Man, it's now or never. I gotta do this." and put some work behind those words.

Chapter 3

VIEWS FROM THE 99%

"If you reach for the moon, you might hit the stars. If you reach for the clouds, you might hit a street pole."

While teaching the importance of developing and maintaining a clear vision, it would be unjust to describe the characteristics of the world's superheroes, aka, the working-class. It's always been crazy to me how the hardest workers in the world, get paid the least, receive the worst benefits, and are still expected to show up without complaint or excuse. Even still, that's precisely what blue-collar workers do. If you asked me which socioeconomic status is comprised of the most loyal people, I'd have to say that it's definitely the middle class! Doing the same thing for thirty years takes a level of commitment that's unprecedented. Showing up with the same level of excellence every year, month, week, down to every weekday, is more than talent. It's intentional perseverance. The pandemic caused by the hands of COVID-19 is a perfect example of workers rolling with the punches to still show up and take care of their homes. Although several policies need to be enacted to make sure we're protecting these workers far better than America has during this shutdown, they still find ways to clock-in and push beyond their limits. Before this, no one could've imagined having to wear latex gloves and a medical mask to work, urging customers to stand six-feet away from each other, limiting occupancy to 25%, and avoiding your family members to keep them safe. But instead of giving up, our essential workers continued to prove that they're the real superheroes of the world. Dedicated to their work, possessing a work-ethic so cold it's sickening, and being literal representations of the word sacrifice. The middle class is the best at taking the little they receive and building a family with it. Imagine taking this same level of drive that you give toward your 9 to 5 and channeling it towards your vision. If anyone can build a family with middle-class salaries, then they can also create a legacy.

I want to be sensitive here, though, because I know struggles with esteem issues are real. So if someone hasn't acknowledged the hard work you've been putting in lately, I want you to know I see you. And maybe, just maybe, one of the reasons you struggle with developing your long-term vision is because systems have done the dreaming for us our entire lives. Elementary school taught you how to dream about middle school. Middle school taught you how to visualize high school. High school took you to college or trade school. Between eighteen and twenty-four, you were cornered into declaring a major and answering what you'd want to do from twenty-five to sixty-five. Once you landed the job that you'd work for two-plus generations, they taught you how to dream inside their corporate system. The middle-class has minimal experience dreaming for itself, and it's evident by looking at our current societal norms. Blue-collar workers didn't dream up six-week maternity leaves, sixty-hour weeks with no overtime, quarter-cent raises and insurance that doesn't cover mental health. Those are the dreams of the owners looking to cut spending at the expense of their workers.

I need you to understand that It doesn't matter if you get paid $4.00/hr or $4,000/hr. If you don't have a vision for your life that involves passive income rolling into your accounts each month, you're enslaved to your job. And we all know how difficult it is to live a full life when you're stressed about maintaining a position that determines your entire livelihood. It's even hard to spend quality time with your loved ones when you're only working to pay the bills and nothing more. Quick reality check, we were meant to live for so much more!

At this point, you know that I refer to my father as Superman. Growing up, I felt like he was this invincible superhuman. Picture it; he was a 6'4 275 lbs man with a mini-afro and sideburns like Shaft, who had a gun on each hip while driving a Cadillac. He was more than a sergeant to me. There was this one time when someone tried to rob his record shop with a gun while I was there. My father handled the robber like it was a regular part of his day. I didn't see an ounce of fear in his eyes—just pure focus and determination as he snatched the gun away and apprehended him. You couple me witnessing my father beat down a bad guy on top of all of our neighbors bringing their daily issues to him; I never imagined him being able to be hurt.

But like every child, the day finally came when I realized my father could hurt just like me. To this day, I don't know the story. All I can remember is coming home and seeing my father had a broken leg. My 6'4 Superman had become Clark Kent on crutches. It was a new reality for me to process. It wasn't like my father lost his worth; he just became human for the first time to me. Looking back, I wonder how our household would've been shaken had my father been so injured he could no longer work. Being a sergeant, it would have been very different from someone's father who worked at the plant. Yet, even the benefits that could've come with my father being a sergeant and potentially having to retire early, our lifestyles could've been drastically different.

My parents' envisioned a home full of children that they would love and protect. To be specific, they wanted four children, two boys, and two girls, a home where the children would go off to school, land their dream jobs and marry their soul mates. My mother wanted working to be an option for her, and it was. She and my father would take yearly vacations for a week to travel. They could drop all four of us off at our grandparents while they used their furlough time together. We had frequent family outings and got to experience the best of middle-class living. Sadly, so much could have been halted had either one of my parents, especially my father, lost their jobs for a significant amount of time.

The saying that multiple streams of income no longer being an option is just as accurate today as

it was back then. But very few people are showing others how they can do it while keeping their
day jobs. In the next part of this chapter, we will
cover some of the myths that blue-collar workers
hold concerning starting up a side-business.

I Can't Start A Business Because...

Misinformation and a lack of self-assessment
drive the working-class into avoiding building
their businesses or side-hustles. It's never been
about ability, intelligence, or any other factor that
these gurus like to talk about online. The blue-
collar community is comprised of the wittiest,
most capable, and dedicated people you'll ever
meet. The bridge between them and the wealthy
are the myths they hold onto because of inaccu-
rate teachings and a lack of exposure.

The first and one of the most lethal myths that
blue-collar workers fall for is, "To build wealth, you
have to come from wealth." According to a report
run by Wealth-X in 2019, only 8.5% of the wealthiest people inherited their wealth ultimately. Only
23.7% of the world's wealthiest inherited part of
the riches and self-generated wealth. Meanwhile,
67.7% of the wealthiest people are classified as
self-made. Meaning, their fortune wasn't gener-
ated by a wealthy family's backing, not that they
worked alone and made every dollar by themselves. Even still, nearly 70% of millionaires don't
come from families that could invest in them,
more than likely, blue-collar backgrounds. Now
we won't paint a fairytale picture here. The majority of these people have other privileges that

allow them to overcome specific societal barriers with far greater ease than minority and disenfranchised communities. But you can't debate facts. If almost 70% of millionaires today came from homes with working parents, there's hope for you.

The next internal lie is believing the greatest asset of life is money. It's hard to think of as a myth, especially when money isn't a free-flowing luxury. Even the Bible says money answereth all things. So what I'm about to say isn't to call the Holy Book a liar. It's to add context to the position of money in our lives. Blue-collar workers are trained to believe that money is the be-all and end-all. In reality, it's time. This is why the wealthy will sacrifice thousands, if not millions of dollars into saving them time. Why? Because the use of time determines your quality of life and how much money you're able to generate. But if you believe money is the center focus, you'll always think you need to give up more time to make more money. I've always wanted to come up with a way to make money without physically having to be there. You need to learn how to do the same. I'm not sure if you've paid attention to it, but doesn't it seem as though the more money people make, the less they have to show up to work? Almost as if they're being rewarded for working less? Well, that's the structure of capitalism. The more you make, the more you're being entrusted to use your mind to solve problems, versus using your physical body to handle administrative and manual labor. So the wealthy understand that the more they can use their intellectual property, the less they have to show up. So it doesn't mean the more money you make, the less hard work you involve yourself in. It just means the way that you work begins to shift and change as you acquire more responsibility. One thing people don't realize is that there's a huge liability that comes with being wealthy. The difference between a person making $20.00/hour versus the person making $250,000 a year, is likely the amount of risk the latter person has to take. So if they can find ways to save them time to be more efficient and effective, they'll be willing to spend the money to get it. It might be the hardest mental-shift when going from a worker's mindset to an owner's mentality. Being afraid of spending the money to make smarter decisions will eventually lead you to pay for expensive repairs later on.

The third myth I'd like to address is this issue of debt. So many people see debt as this devil waiting to catch them by their feet. Because of the woes of struggling to pay off student loan debt and credit cards opened while being young and impressionable; liability has one of the worst emotional connections. But like everything else, debt can be used as a tool to build wealth and create a crazy impact. Take Pixar; for example, in their documentary they discuss how they were going under by at least a million dollars in their first five years i. But they continued to work on Pixar's team, lay their foundations, and eventually, they released Toy Story, which made them $39.1 million within the first five days of its release. Their early investors had to trust in the vision to continue pouring into the company, but if you ask me, ever since the release of Toy Story, Pixar has yet to flop. In a more relatable example, debt can be used to help you secure your first investment property. When I purchased my first investment property I was able to leverage the overall debt. I did this by providing quality housing to renters who in return, paid me enough in payments to not only pay back the bank what I borrowed, but also receive $3,000 net income every month for taking on the debt. The only difference between a debt being a source of pain and a resourceful tool is the use of applicable information.

The last set of negative frameworks we're going to cover is centered on character. The number of times I've heard people say things like:

"All business owners are greedy."
"Anybody that owns a business is shady."
"Wealthy people don't care about people."
"Wealthy people aren't happy."
"Wealthy people are evil."
"The wealthy should give away all their money and pay more."
"You don't even need all that money to be happy."
"All the wealthy care about is money."
"How much money is too much money?"

All of the preceding statements are absolutely ridiculous. First, people always misinterpret the scriptures to try and make the accumulation of money this obscene act before God. The text never said money is the root of all evil. It speaks to the love of money being the root of all evil, and we've seen that through all of history. From the Trans-Atlantic slave trade to WWII, we know of the love of money at the center of these historical events. However, trying to compare everyone who's ever made a substantial amount of money to the likes of Hitler or even the 45th President is ridiculous. Solomon was noted as the wealthiest man ever. MSN stated that if Solomon's wealth were brought into today, it would be worth $2.2 trillion dollars.

Solomon is noted as the wisest man ever to exist and a king of Israel, the nation of God's choosing. You might be familiar with his downfall, but my point is that riches aren't the defining factor for someone's character. Being rich doesn't make you the devil's handyman, and being poor doesn't make you a saint. There is no humility attached to not being able to take care of your home or family. There is no special prize attached to avoiding wealth building so that you can intentionally live a harder life. Money doesn't automatically equate to happiness, but it sure does buy the things that add to it. No matter how far away you run from money, it'll always be there because we live in a world run by capitalism. That house costs money. That car costs money. Your children's food costs money, and so does their education, even in public school. It takes money to clothe them and yourself. That trip you've wanted to take costs money, and it takes money to enjoy yourself while you're there, not just to book the departure ticket. If I had to encourage you to tackle any of these false beliefs first, I'd honestly say to start here. We can't make smart money decisions if we continually look at it, and the people that have it like they're the cause of our misfortunes. You have too much power to be bound by low-level thinking.

The entire point of this book is to help redefine what's possible for blue-collar workers. The caveat is that I can't do the work for you. I've served my twenty plus years to building, teaching and raising It's time for you to put in your years of refining now. You can work your job, build a business, raise a family (if that's what you want), be a fantastic spouse (again, if that's what you desire), travel and have a great time. And despite everything that some of these top business publications share, the process is a hell of a lot simpler than we make it.

MILLIONAIRE MOMENTS

What are the myths you've been holding onto? When you think back on the times you've said you couldn't make any more money or be a better person, what were your beliefs?

After taking a moment to reflect, feel free to write down your answer somewhere safe and you can even share it with me by sending me a message on Instagram: @9to5millionaire

Big Little Lies

Resetting your state of mind so you can create a new vision for yourself will take way more self-reflection than you might think. There's a virus in society telling you that you have to live a certain kind of way. You're only supposed to spend x amount of time with your children and spouse, and you're only allowed to live for this time. It's a societal virus that dictates the norm for everyone that will enable it to overtake them. Be honest, based on the way you're living and thinking, compared to what everyone else is doing around you, do you have it?

What are the norms and beliefs that currently guide your decisions and, ultimately, your reality? While answering that question, I need you to be honest with yourself. There is a big difference between being real with yourself and beating yourself up. This isn't a moment of pity. It's a time to analyze the big little lies you've been fed and are currently feeding yourself.

The vaccine for the societal virus has always been not caring about what it told me to believe. Do you think a Black man from Chicago, raised by officers, called a nigger throughout his foundational years, known for fighting the biggest and the baddest, only exposed to blue-collar jobs should have the audacity that I have to go after what I want? I'm just like everyone else when it comes to life hitting me upside my head. There were several times when my dream didn't go as planned, times I met one of the bad guys, moments I was encouraged to dream smaller, but I don't have an ounce of care for any of these moments. Why? Because I know what I want and I always do the necessary work to get it. I go above and beyond to ensure the vision I have for my life is consistently manifesting itself.

So the doubting questions you usually ask yourself, I want you to replace them with, "Will I be
able to live with the choices I make?" If the answer isn't an immediate yes, then the choice isn't
worth it. Let this guide your vision! How you treat
people, the things you'll do for your family, the
places you want to go, the types of people you
want to meet, the jobs you accept—can you live
with these for the rest of your life?

Remember, you've been programmed to focus
on delayed gratification so much that it might be
hard to even envision life's pleasures as something tangible for the near future. You're stepping into the 1% zone now, though. You deserve
to build wealth now and enjoy the fruits of your
labor simultaneously. This isn't a call to immature
decision making. This is a declaration that you
should enjoy your days on this earth as much as
you work on making it a better place for everyone else.

While you're dreaming, you must separate yourself from your current reality. Yes, race, gender,
socioeconomic status and access can be limitations placed on you by the world. But in the inner
world that's owned, managed, created, and con-
trolled by your thoughts, you have to see yourself
capable of receiving everything you want. Once
you're done dreaming, you wake up and put in
the work to make it a reality. If you sleep for eight
hours, work for nine; you still have seven hours
left...don't tell me you don't have time for your
family, to learn about investing, budgeting or to
set-up an LLC. So dream big and start working
smarter!

MINDSET

Chapter 4

ALL-STAR

I left grammar school feeling like the man. Despite the challenges with my skin color, I became the strongest, smartest, most capable student walking those halls. But like every thirteen-year old, my freshman year reminded me that I was just a small fish in a big pond again. A new place meant for conquering (if you were capable of showing up well). I was Jemal in grammar school, but walking into my ninth grade year, I became Tommie's little brother. Everything I could brag about in middle school was now considered average or expected. Initially, it took me by surprise. All the years before, I just needed to show up to be great. But now, I had to learn what hard work really meant.

You remember the feeling; that first test, that first try-out, or even the first homework assignment that tested what you knew about yourself. Because the high school landscape is so different, I had to learn that the level of talent had shifted quickly. I was cold for my age, but I wasn't the best compared to the vets, aka upper-classmen. I had room for improvement in every area of my life, and it was a humbling experience.

Once I realized the shifts I would have to make to catch-up (although not behind), I started reshaping my actions to meet the vision I had set for myself at eight. Being reminded that I had to work harder didn't throw me off my course; if anything, it helped bring a level of realism to my dreams. Remember when I told the story of wanting to be a millionaire in grammar school? By the time I was ten or maybe even eleven, I decided that football would be the vehicle I used to get me to my million dollar status. Soon as I made my mind-up on football, I started training and visualizing my future NFL career.

The downside was not being able to play the sport on a school team for years. Because everyone Black was bussed in, we had to head back to our communities as soon as school was over. Not a single Black person stayed after school. So for years, I had to work at something I couldn't even officially claim to be a part of because of an obstacle that counted me out because of my race. I'd like to take a minute to pause and remind you as a reader that the worst parts of this nation aren't as far away as you might think. I'm only forty-two while writing this book. That's a reality I had to face as a child. So never think someone's story about dealing with the brutality of racism sounds too far-fetched in (whatever year it is you're reading this). I didn't experience something as extreme as getting killed for being Black; however, before I knew geometry, I had been repeatedly called a nigger, forced to fight, and kept out of sports because of the color of my skin; not my character.

Back to topic.

I remember choosing football as my career be-cause that's all I had access to viewing. Now, of course, I wasn't consciously aware that I was making that decision based on my level of ex-posure. But in the eighties, there weren't many Black TV shows, and you didn't see a bunch of people that looked like you outside of the Cosby Show and Good Times. And even with their in-fluence, you never really knew how much money they made as actors. The Black people you saw flexing in their cars, being in the dopest com-mercials, were professional athletes. In particular, football players and basketball players. It wasn't like today where you can log onto Instagram and follow accounts like @9to5Millionaire (obviously I have to plug myself) and see people that look just like you living lavish lifestyles and being mor-ally sound. It was a very different landscape back then, and the only thing I knew for sure was that working a city job wasn't going to make me the millionaire I desired to be. The occurrence that confirmed my decision to play professionally was my trip to train with The National Champions - the Michigan Wolverines. After my trip, I knew I could go all the way even though I wasn't ob-sessed with the actual sport. I focused on the fi-nancial outcome.

You might be wondering how my family, specifi-cally my parents (who worked in law enforce-ment and had three kids aspiring to be educa-tors and officers), felt about me telling them I wanted to be an NFL player. Looking back, they were okay with my decision. I was truly blessed to have parents who meant what they said when they encouraged me to be anything I wanted. They didn't necessarily understand my decision, but they never gave me any pushback. Mainly because my grind matched my words, they would remind me that I could do anything, but I had to be the best. So that's precisely what I became.

The Start Of A Dream

All of those years of dreaming, anticipating, training and visualizing were finally used during my freshman year of high school when I made the football and baseball team (which I played freshman through junior year). From ten to fourteen, my only option was to train with neighbors and play in outside leagues. Being able to be on my first school team felt like a small (very small) reward of the work I had been putting in. I didn't let it make my head big, though, because the goal wasn't to become a freshman-level football player. It was to make it to the league and play long enough to secure the life of my dreams.

I was so focused, that I even sacrificed my sixteenth birthday party for football. Giving up a birthday party might not be a big thing for some, but in my family, we celebrated sixteenth birthdays like a coming of age party. Each kid got to host the biggest party that they've had up to date, and our parents would invite all of our friends to come and celebrate us. There'd be plenty of food, music, dancing and games. A dream for a sixteen-year-old.

Except for me.

When my parents asked me what I'd like to do to commemorate becoming a young adult, I told them that I'd like to attend one of the most popular football camps in the world. They were stunned. It was a family rite of passage to have a King Birthday Bash. Instead, I asked them to ship me off to the University of Michigan football camp to learn drills, go against some of the top football players in the country, and be seen by potential coaches.

What they didn't realize was that I didn't think I deserved the party. I've always felt like you need something worth celebrating to throw a party, which should've been the fact that I was turning a year older. But that felt small after getting the news that I got benched on the football team. This $500 camp was going to help me not only earn my spot back but secure it. I was out for blood . Getting benched ignited a level of competitiveness in me that I hadn't had to use before.

So I went off to the camp. I trained non-stop for days. I got to compete with the top athletes. I learned about my skill gaps and what areas I dominated. We got nutrition lessons, worked on strength training, agility and explosiveness. By the time I came back home, I knew I wasn't average anymore. This new confidence and skill set showed up on the field, and I went from being benched to starting, to team captain and moved up to varsity within the first few games. Missing out on a party was well worth the sacrifice. That's why I tell people all the time, 'If you want different, you have to do different.' The level of exposure that I received by training with the national champions was absolutely life changing!

Decisions like that one are what got me recognized by my coaches too. I might not have been the best on the baseball team, but I was undoubtedly the hardest working, the same thing for football (although I was also a top contender here). I was a captain for both sports teams because I was focused on a goal that was years away, it wasn't about just winning a measly high school football championship. I never let myself grow comfortable. While others were eating during lunch, I hurried off to the gym to work on some techniques and get a quick workout before eating afterward. Even at the end of practice, you'd find me making additional sprints to push myself mentally. Sometimes my teammates would hop in with me; other times, it was just me and the turf. I took that championship mentality instilled in me at Michigan and displayed it everyday during high school. Every athlete knows that 70% of your sport is your mental strength. Consistently sacrificing was turning me into a beast not to be contended with.

This fight carried on throughout high school. Despite my grades being pretty average (I had a 2.7

GPA), I was still treated as one of the top students in my class. I carried my weight, I never intentionally missed class, I wasn't caught up in the drama, I was cool with people of all races, and I almost always took the higher ground. You couple that with my athleticism, and I was a natural-born leader. And I know I got this from my upbringing. Consistency, problem-solving, dedication and determination are all blue-collar attributes. I remember when my high school counselor Ms. Penny told me that there was something different about me. I ran into her later in life, and she said she wasn't wrong about me. That brought a smile to my face.

My deep-seated desire for anything different drove me to use all of the lessons that my parents taught me. Plus, taking in all of the teachings by watching how everyone else was living their lives helped me avoid dumb decisions early on. I knew that if I acted like I was in college while I was in high school, I'd always be on top of my game. Honestly, I moved like this to make sure when it was time for graduation; I didn't feel like a little fish in a big pond again. Throughout high school, I didn't even feel like I was there. It was a never-ending game of me wanting to be the standout kid and relying on my good character and work ethic to make sure that was my reality. I had some support in doing that, too, from someone that I still love very deeply.

High School Sweetheart

Like the majority of successful men, I'm a married man. The ways that my marriage has shaped the longevity of my success is an entire book. But for now, we'll focus on how we met.

Going into my third year, I had the option of choosing a woodshop or art class. Our football coach Robert Jurka who taught wood shop and who would later tell me before his passing that I was going to one day be overly successful in life, also told me that I should marry my high school sweetheart Camille. I knew I'd spend most of my time with Coach anyway, So I chose art. I was sitting at a table on the first day of class as a junior, and she sat directly next to me. I asked her for her name, and she casually told me, 'Camille.' And instantly, after we exchanged names, we began talking about our interests, what we thought the class was going to be like and if either one of us liked art. There was no flirting, and not an ounce of her seemed to be enthralled by me. We talked so much that the teacher threatened to move me to woodshop class. That didn't stop us from cracking jokes, though. As promised, I ended up getting moved just because Camille and I would not stop talking during class. We became immediate friends. But like most sixteen-year-old boys, I was dating someone already. So Camille and I grew into friends because that's all we could be. I've never been a man to disrespect women or boundaries. But there was just something about Camille that made her a great friend.

We would talk for hours updating each other on the day, debating topics, checking in on each other's families, and more. This was cool to me because, by my junior year, I was a star player. Most of the girls would act weird around me. Not Camille, though. She cared less about how successful a football player I was. She had her own accolades.

She was faith-filled, family-focused, and one of the smartest people I knew in school. Kid you not, I met Camille when she was thirteen and a high school sophomore (she skipped a grade in elementary school). She graduated high school by the time she was sixteen! The woman did not play about her schooling. By the time I was a senior, I knew she was the young lady I wanted to pursue. She never chased after me. We never felt pressured into being anything other than friends, but because of the vision I had early on, I knew she was a gem and worth the pursuit. She was different from the women I frequently saw. And you know how I feel about being different at this point.

By the time we started dating, it was the most natural relationship I'd been in because we were friends first. I respected her and vice versa. She consistently supported me and reminded me to go hard for the things I wanted. She always pushed me to show up as my best self.

So much so, she came to her first football game only to watch me play during homecoming. I had three touchdowns that game, and we won. I made sure we didn't waste her time. The hardest part of our relationship was the age difference. Not for any crazy reason, but because of prom. For my senior prom, we couldn't go together because her mother said she was too young. However, the deal was for me to return the next year and take her to hers. I kept well on my promise.

Changing Ponds

By my senior year, I had everything I needed for the next season of my life. I had a girlfriend I could trust. I was a top recruit in Illinois. I was all-conference, city, and state. I had the privilege of playing in jersey #99; a jersey passed down from the best player to the next. I was receiving co-signs from coaches and being offered collegiate scholarships all over the country. I was ready to transition into a new pond.

At graduation, I was named most popular, athletic, and likely to succeed by my peers all over again. I can vividly remember how excited everyone was for my next season of life. The administration and faculty made sure I knew that I was loved and proud of me. By the time I reached the graduation stage, I was ready to move forward with my life. I was yet another step closer to my goal of being a millionaire.

As I prepared during my last summer pre-college, I trained like a mad man. Ironically enough, it was the hottest summer we'd ever had. We were reaching 95-degrees on average in Chicago! I was used to negative degrees, but 90° weather was a beast I hadn't been introduced to. I had to wake up at 4 am to train in 85° weather. To add context to how crazy this weather was, we had over 700 deaths in Chicago that summer because of the heatwave. But no matter how hot it was, I had to keep showing up. I kept thinking about how drastic the transition was from eighth to ninth grade and wanted to be prepared for entering a new world. Honestly, this was the first time I felt nervous about going off to a university. Because I was so vocal about my plans, everyone knew what my goal was. So they'd see me and ask how training was going and if I thought I was ready. It was no longer just my dream. It was a community mission.

So when it was time to pack my bags and head off to Western Illinois University, I wasn't going because of my own might. I was going with the influence of those that helped raise me and a vision for the future. Luckily, I had Camille (after she went to community college for a year at age sixteen because of her mother's insistence, so I wasn't alone. But college ended up being exactly what I had been preparing for. I planned on finishing my credits needed for a degree and getting drafted my senior year. I know most young men would've taken the first opportunity to dip, but I knew how significant that degree was to my family. We were raised to esteem higher education, and I didn't feel like explaining to my mother why I didn't finish a free education.

All four and a half years, I focused on the next step; draft day. Nothing about my work-ethic changed. I remained focused and clear on my end-goal, which, again, wasn't to be a professional football player. It was to be wealthy. Not a single time did I confuse the role of the NFL, and I definitely wasn't trying to create a plan B. Plan B was to strategize how to make method A work. Something that so many blue-collar workers don't quite get yet.

Your Vehicle Isn't Your Destination

When I ask people what they want to be, they almost always respond with what they want to do. I'll ask them the question, and they'll respond by saying:

"I want to be a nurse."

"I want to become a writer."

"I want to be an entrepreneur."

And then I have to rephrase the question for them. See, being something and doing something are very different. Sadly, most of us grew up in cultures that define you by what makes you your money. When you meet someone, what are the first two questions that you ask them?

"What's your name?"

"What do you do?"

Based on their answers, we'll determine the level of importance they hold and whether we'd like to associate ourselves with them. Don't lie either. We've all done it. Going back to the degree analogy we used in previous chapters, it's the same context here. We raise workers, train them to be better workers, and define them by the work they accomplish. If they go out and get additional letters behind their name, they become even more valuable workers.

We never ask children how they want to live growing up. We certainly don't ask them the type of people they want to mature into. We confuse their being with their *doing'* before they're old enough to distinguish between them. So they evolve into full-grown adults that genuinely believe their highest sense of worth is what keeps the food on their tables. Not their character, not their interests, nor their secret aspirations. Jobs become their identity, which is why many fall into a deep depression upon retirement because not only are they retiring from their careers but also their identities. You were taught that you are who you are, as a whole person, and your titles are just extensions of you. This is probably why bosses become self-obsessed and managers forget what it's like to work on the ground level.

Think of Career Day as an example. There is no Destination Day. This is why so many blue-collar workers are depressed at work and resent their positions because they've made their vehicle their destination. It's not even their fault that they did; that's how we've been trained. Imagine, as a kid, if your parents told you for spring break we are going to take a trip to the car! That wouldn't make sense to a five-year-old, and it definitely shouldn't make sense to an adult. When they were four, eight, twelve and eighteen, they got asked the wrong question. They were asked about a job, not a destination. They've been hoodwinked and don't even know it. Without knowing how to separate the two, they've been taught to put pressure on a vehicle meant for a destination. Imagine if someone would ask us as children how we want to live versus how we intend to work for the rest of our lives. Maybe the number of people who obtain higher education and decide not to use their degrees would be smaller. Possibly there'd be fewer people walking around anticipating their breaking points.

Here's the core of understanding your vehicle versus your destination.

Your vehicle is what gets you to your destination. It's the job, the investment property, the new business, the insurance plan—its sole purpose is to guide you to your intended outcome. It's what drives you, or even flies, sails, or runs you to the different mile-points in your overall vision for your life. The issue with understanding this is separating who you are with what you do. You're a whole being outside of your vehicle(s).

Whole.

All they do is attest to where you're headed, which is why I can look at what you're currently doing and tell you where you'll be in ten years. You've always been in the vehicle; you just might not have been the one driving. The driver could be your company or family. But if you've never separated the two, I can promise there's something or someone else that's been steering the vehicle for you.

Your destination is how you plan on living in the future. It encompasses your dreams, passions and desires. It answers the following:

Where do you want to live?

How much money do you want to make a year at the minimum?

Do you want to travel? If so, where and how frequently?

Do you want to be married?

Do you want to have kids?

What mission trips do you want to go on?

How will you serve your community?

How will you be known in your neighborhood?

What are your core values?

What characteristics define you?

How much money do you want to be considered a small gesture when you give it away?

Do you plan on tithing?

What do you do for fun?

What does an average week look like for you?

What does an ordinary vacation look like?

Do you cook your meals, or do you take out? What about a chef? Do you order meal preps?

What does an extravagant vacation look like?

What type of people are in your circle?

How many friends do you have?

How much will you have saved by (insert age)?

Do you plan on retiring? If so, when?

Do you do the cleaning or is there someone else that you hire?

What does retirement look like for you?

What are ten crazy things on your bucket list? How do you train yourself mentally?

What types of books and publications do you read?

Your destination paints a picture of the type of lifestyle you want to create. At no point is it focused on the kind of jobs you'll have in the process. That's totally up to you. But the dream that you paint for yourself will determine which vehicles are most efficient.

You can't pick the right vehicle without knowing the exact destination. You can't use a car to get from Illinois to Israel. Most people choose destinations without realistic vehicles and get frustrated that they aren't going where they thought they were. To help you gain clarity, let's outline your destination right now.

Look at the questions above and use those to guide you as you write out your life's vision in a place you won't lose it. There is no right or wrong answer or length here. Don't stop writing until you can see it, feel it, smell it and taste it. Once you finish, come back to this section and complete the next exercise.

Your Potential Vehicles

If you haven't noticed, the vehicle above was intentionally written in the plural. The reason is that each vehicle represents a different stream of income. And what did we say about only having one stream in the last chapter? That one is too close to having none—right! Unless your destination is small and short-lived, you'll need various forms of transportation to get there. This is where your current job comes into play.

Because although you can't get to Israel from Illinois with a car, you can use it to get you to the airport. Then that plane will land and it'll take you to another vehicle or a bus or even a train. But the point to focus on is that it's going to take more than one, but if you know where you're headed, you'll know what kind of vehicles are needed to get there. The reason why I was so focused on football as a kid was that I was intending on it being my private jet. It was dependable and it would require a lot of sacrifices to obtain it, but it would directly land me in the millionaire realm. I've noticed that some people aren't willing to get to their destination because they don't immediately know how to get a Lamborghini as their vehicle. Every good vehicle is a vehicle that moves.

Having a vehicle that moves slowly isn't your issue. It's your inability to see where that vehicle can get you, and what vehicle makes the most sense to acquire next. In other words, your job probably isn't a problem with achieving your dreams. It's your perspective. The way I made it to my first destination was by using the following:

Officer = my Toyota Camry

Real Estate = my private jet

Daycares = my yacht

Security Company = my bullet train

We'll discuss why football isn't listed in chapter five. But as you can see, I used each vehicle to make me a multi-millionaire, and each of them came in the order listed above (investment types not included). Even more importantly, they came naturally! When you're picking vehicles, you shouldn't pick anything that feels like a considerable force. Being an officer introduced me to real estate. Real estate brought the daycare opportunity. The daycares opened up the security company. You should never get another vehicle until that first vehicle can afford the next one. Make the first one work before investing your time and money into another stream. Leverage one stream then add another. With that said, don't just drop a vehicle because you find success in another one. You can keep both. Two is always better than one because two can withstand the stresses of life. Abandoning your first vehicle adds the pressure of two onto the one, creating more stress to your now unstable foundation.

For my extremists out there, remember that you can't start it all at once. Each stream is going to require life adjustments, time adjustments, potentially hiring on teams and other big steps. One successful stream will always lead to another one, and they'll have opportunities to create smaller vehicles inside them. Go all-in on each before you move forward. And of course, give each the necessary amount of time needed to become successful. If it's not working, ask what you're doing wrong. More than likely you're not doing something correctly. Very rarely (if ever) is it the vehicle. People are out here shipping potatoes to college students with custom messages written on them, and it's a million-dollar company. Vehicles, no matter how ridiculous, work if you know how to drive them.

It's also imperative that you know the difference between your vehicles and your destination so you won't get tricked into stopping once you acquire the next vehicle. If real estate were my end goal, I would've stopped at my first property, and that would've been scary because I wouldn't have opened a daycare nor the security company. If anything happened to me, and I no longer was able to go into work as an officer and couldn't work in real estate, my family's life would look very different. If one or two vehicles break down, it shouldn't have total control over your life. This is the upper hand the wealthy have on the middle-class. The rich get richer because they know how to invest and what their destinations are. Nobody tells the wealthy what they want except themselves. But the wealthy tell the middle and lower class what they should want, how they should think and what vehicles would work. Money dictates *everything* that they decide. That's why mastering this concept is so vital! Who's driving you right now?

MILLIONAIRE MOMENTS

What have you been calling your destination but it was really just a vehicle?

What was your biggest "aha moment" while reading this chapter?

How are you feeling now that you know the difference between the vehicle and the destination?

What are three things you plan on teaching your loved ones about this concept?

What are some immediate changes you plan on making?

After taking a moment to reflect, feel free to write down your answer somewhere safe and you can even share it with me by sending me a message on Instagram: @9to5millionaire.

Chapter 5

THE WAKE-UP CALL

If you were paying close attention during the last chapter, you might've asked how I went from training for the NFL to being an officer and using my other streams as vehicles. Despite how I looked, I never did make it to the NFL. I know, crazy. What they say about one percent of top players getting drafted a year is correct. Here's how my story went.

I remember waking up every morning, getting my mind ready for AM practice before class. It was a process of making sure I made it to check-in on time, getting to the weight room by 4:30 AM, rushing to shower post-workout, getting to team breakfast, and finally rushing off to class. By the time most regular students woke up for school, I had completed more than what they would complete all day! By the middle of the day, we either had tutor check-ins or afternoon skills training and another workout. In the evening, we'd go over the film from previous games to prepare for an upcoming one. I didn't know it then, but I was a full-time employee for Western, which is why I never understood the idea that athletes have it easier in school. Student-athletes live two very complicated lives. On one end, they're excelling in their sport to remain on the team and passing their classes to stay at the university (even if only to remain eligible), while intentionally positioning themselves to be seen by professional coaches. Every game, just like every exam for traditional students, either gains you another point or takes away points on your draft day board. There's very little room to be lazy, no matter how talented you are.

Like many other athletes at my school, I thought about the professional league frequently. It was a part of our chants, our mottos and our expectations. If you would've asked me if I ever thought about not making it to the NFL, I would've said never. I didn't have time to think about not making it. There was too much work to do to get there in the first place. Some people call that wishful thinking, maybe even unrealistic, but when you're betting on yourself to be a part of that top one percent, wondering if you're capable isn't worth your time. You train to make it. You recover so you can train again. You eat so you can work more. Everything you do is done with intention. This also wasn't 2020 when athletes were being encouraged to think about plan B's. Playing football at a Division I (D1) school like Western required total buy-in. That means your mental, emotional, spiritual, and physical states all had to agree to the mission. And our mission was to draft as many of us as possible.

Thinking about it, football consumed every part of us. My teammates were majority D1 transfers looking to play at a school known for getting players to the league. I was one of the few players on the team that got to Western immediately out of high school. Before every intense workout, our coaches would ask us, "Who's going to the league?" All committed to excellence; every single player raised their hands. Shoot, even my junior year felt like a sign of God. The Rams came to practice at our school for preseason training camp. We used the same fields, weight rooms and dorms. They felt like an extension of us, our older and professional big brothers. It didn't help that this would be the same year they'd win the Superbowl!

You can imagine what it was like on draft day then. After deciding at eight that I wanted to be a millionaire and choosing football as my vehicle at ten, I'd dedicated a decade of my life to preparing for that very moment. I wasn't alone in my commitments either. My parents got me to and from practice as a teenager. My siblings would support me at my games. Other family members and neighbors found ways to help me too. I didn't get to Western by my merit alone. I got there because of my hard work and the support of my tribe. These are the people that would be in my home as we turned on the TV to watch the draft.

Day one went by, and we were hopeful. Day two went by, and we felt a little anxious, but hope hadn't died. But when day three ended, and I hadn't received a call, I was disappointed. For the first time, I hadn't accomplished a goal. I felt weird, less than, betrayed by myself, and my dreams and goals. For the first time, I had felt like a failure. But my hope hadn't died out completely. There was still the option of landing a tryout. So I switched my mindset to that to finish the semester out with a little peace.

The draft had passed on, and graduation day had come. I'm sure it was supposed to feel like a time of bliss, even accomplishment. But I felt like I only received half of what I went to school for. Honestly, more than half because I only stayed because of football and my family. When I first got there, I don't remember my major, I just know I started as Pre-Law and made my way to Sociology after some time. Why exactly? Who knows. I wasn't going to be a sociologist. I don't even know what sociologists do. But I had stuck to the family motto and gotten my degree after being there for four and a half years. But because it was a requirement, it had been just another graduation. As soon as I finished walking, they asked me when I was heading off to get my master's. And you know why. With every certificate or degree came an increase in pay.

The issue was, I never planned on working a traditional job. My goal was to become a millionaire by playing a professional sport. I had no intention of using my plan B.

Post-Traumatic Sports Disorder

The hardest part about coping was there not being a shift in my day-to-day. My body didn't change because I didn't get drafted. The amount of food I ate in a day didn't shift. My environment didn't immediately turn. My workouts remained the same. People's expectations of me playing pro-ball didn't disappear. Everything took a crazy amount of time just to readjust to my new reality.

For most of my time in transition, I would have thoughts like, "I was almost at the front door of my dreams, and then, the door disappeared." Seriously, what do you do when your vehicle disappoints you? A vehicle you once saw for yourself, you now had to watch your friends ride off into the sunset in. I remember going through a period of asking myself how certain people made it, why I wasn't chosen and what I could have done differently. It wasn't pettiness either. I just couldn't rationalize it. There's no class called "How To Process Disappointment." Naturally, I started to feel like I could no longer attain my million-dollar destination because my vehicle stopped working. I was suffering like most former athletes from what I coined post traumatic sports disorder.

I believe there should be counseling offered to student-athletes specifically for moments like this. Day in and out, you beat your body to make it your slave. You defy the odds mentally. You become a beast. Then one day, you look up, go pro or graduate and get a regular job. For the first time, you're not expected to use your body's athleticism. You're regular now. But because you haven't changed, you still feel like the beast you've been training for. It's easy to say, "Just transfer that energy over into your career." when you haven't experienced it, but it's a startling life change. Some students graduate and go through post-grad depression because for the first time since they were three, they're no longer identified as students, it's the same for athletes. Any time you take away a piece of someone's identity they shake, some fall, and some even break. This is the danger of defining yourself as your vehicle instead of your characteristics. When the vehicle changes, you think you've lost a part of yourself.

Drafted To The Force

So like any self-fulfilling prophecy, I got drafted to the police force upon graduating. Ironically enough, the year I completed my degree was the same year they were vetting new officers. I say ironically because the force doesn't take on new people every year. People hear my story and ask me why I didn't decide to play for the XFL or Canadian ball. They don't realize my love wasn't for football; it was for my end-goal. And the XFL and Canadian leagues were paying as much as the Chicago Police Department. So if I had to join a team, I would prefer the one that didn't promise concussions and broken ribs.

Transitioning in was pretty swift. My dad had been pushing me for a while, and my mother confirmed that it would be a great idea if things didn't work out in my favor. Before we graduated, my best friend and I went to take the test together. This was the start of my coping by buying into the American dream.

Little did I know that the training was going to be a hell of a ride.

It was fifteen weeks of training with eight hour days. The trainees' wore a blue sweater with our names printed across our chests, accompanied by matching blue jogging pants. I had traded in one uniform for the next. The only difference is that for the first time during training, I was pissed, wondering why I was there and analyzing my life. But because my name is King, I still felt a sense of pride because of our family legacy. I'd be walking through the halls, and people would recognize my last name and ask if I was related to the Sergeant King. Moments like that would make me happy despite battling with the idea of becoming an officer.

Remember the PTSD I told you about earlier? Well, my routine didn't change just because I was in a training camp. While the other officers were getting to know each other during our breaks, I would go off and get in another workout. I wanted to make sure I was still ready if I finally got my call, partly because I didn't want to get caught into the routine of the job. My colleagues were cool people, but I've always been interested in keeping my routines no matter what's going on. During the downtime that I wasn't training, I was picking up a new habit of reading. Up until then, I only read to meet education requirements. I didn't even know what the concept of professional development was. But learning new habits to keep sane while becoming an officer wasn't weird.. Reading seemed like the best thing for me because I needed help working on my mental state. By the time I got in the groove of training, working out, and reading, it was officially time for my ceremony.

The Graduation That Mattered

The ceremony you experience before you become an officer is similar to a commencement ceremony. It's called the 'swearing-in,' aka star ceremony. Generations of officers come together to recognize your commitment to your community and service. For me, I had the support of my parents and their friends. It was an honor to be pinned by my dad. Even the Mayor of Chicago was there to honor us. My family was excited about what I had accomplished.

Not to make it sound like they didn't care about my past endeavors. They were proud of me and all of my siblings. But I had finally done something that they could relate to. I had become an officer for the Chicago Police Department, a feat forty-year-olds coveted. Plus, my brother was already serving, so it felt like a cherry on top for me to join the force. Especially to be joining the same one as our father. I was even at the same police station my mother used to check-in as a crossing guard. Never in my life have I seen them applaud the way they applauded, smile the way they smiled, bragged the way they bragged, until that day. I was carrying on the family tradition. For them, I had picked the right team.

There were times I contemplated whether or not I was making the right choice during the ceremony. On what was supposed to be one of the happiest days of my life, I felt like that little boy going from grammar school to high school again. I didn't know what these new waters all entailed, and I wasn't sure if I was supposed to be there in the first place.

But the reality was that I earned my right to be an officer for the Chicago Police Department. And even though I was still suffering from accepting the loss of my first vehicle, I was blessed to have another one. That was the biggest lesson of that time for me. Sometimes your vehicle won't look the way you want it to. I was expecting to be driving a Ferrari to my dreams, and I got a Toyota Camry. Yet, I still had access to the Camry, which meant I still had a chance at my goals. What I've grown to realize is peoples' pride will make them complacent, rather than maneuvering into a vehicle they didn't ask for. They have no idea their first vehicle could lead them to a boat if they took the time to be grateful and strategize.

Eventually, I'd learn the second point for myself, but the first thing I knew was that I had to keep moving. So I got the job, I got engaged to the woman of my dreams, and after some time; I was finally able to accept that I was a part of the Chicago Police Department. That's when I got comfortable.

The job was always interesting, to say the least.

Throughout my shift, I was referred to as King, and they'd always talk about how I looked like I was supposed to be playing for somebody's team. It's still pretty funny to me. The level of physical fitness you had to maintain while being an officer wasn't nearly as close to how in shape I was. With all my mass of being 6'3 220 lbs back then, you'd think I'd get sent out to the dangerous calls. Unlike everyone else on the force, my big sister was my dispatcher. She joined the Chicago Police Department to use the money to pay for her education for her to be a teacher. But in the meantime, we were working together.

My sister Karla worked nights as a dispatcher for the City of Chicago and occasionally she would work my specific zone. There would be times she would try to shield me from potentially dangerous calls. She would try to send me to easy calls, however, you could never be sure. Trust, I had no problems avoiding the potentially life-threatening calls either. I was a newlywed and preferred knowing I would make it home to see my wife, unlike many others. Until one night, I almost didn't make it back.

Sixteen Shots and a Wake-Up Call

On August 18, 2000 (a day I will never forget) my sister dispatched my partner and I to a routine curfew call to make sure some underage kids made it back home since it was after midnight. Typically we'd get out the car, check on them, see where they lived, and escort them home or drive

78

them there. It was always presumed this would be a safe call due to us working with minors.

As my partner and I headed that way, we talked about everything we needed to do that day. At no point did either of us feel eerie about where we were headed or what we were assigned to do. The night was as regular as always.

When we pulled up, we parked the car, walked up to the kids underneath the street light, and asked them why they were out so late and they needed a ride home. Because it's required for us to do a pat-down on each kid before letting them in our squad car, we proceeded to do so. But once I made it to a specific kid, he pushed me and ran off into a dark alley by us. For me, it was game time. I finally got to put my athleticism to use and use my police training for some real action.

Instantly I began to chase behind in the dark alleyway. Running between objects and keeping my focus on the moving body ahead of me, I felt prepared to corner the kid and see why he ran off in the first place. Soon as I made it a few meters behind him, he began to hop the fence topped with barbed wire but was unable to make it over in enough time to get away from me. I thought we were done. The kid thought differently.

He proceeded to pull out his gun that had been tucked in his waistband. As soon as I saw the weapon, I grabbed the barrel as the kid started to let the bullets fly. We were in a tug of war of sorts. I couldn't let go of the gun no matter how much the barrel was burning my hand because he'd be able to shoot me. The kid knew he couldn't just let go because I'd apprehend him. Both of our lives were on a balance-string, but for very different reasons. Then out of nowhere, my partner shows up in the alley behind us. He couldn't see me because of the lighting, so he assumed the fire was for him. Little did he know when he began to shoot back, that he was firing directly in my way. Pissed wasn't the word. Amid this kid letting off what felt like non-stop rounds, I was also dodging bullets from my partner until he finally heard my voice. The phrase, 'being stuck between a rock and a hard place' couldn't even compare to the circumstance I was placed in. Most people are still going through training after only being on their jobs for two months. But sixty days on the police force and I was in a near-death experience.

After sixteen shots were let off, the kid managed to get away, and we were left in a potentially morbid situation. Shock ran through my body as the other officers pulled up after being alerted of the shootout. I was processing if I got hit, if my partner was okay, and what just happened. But this was a job. There was no time to figure out those kinds of pleasantries. Once the officers were there, we were alerted that bullets had gone into the apartment complex on the other side of where we were. Not only had I almost lost my life, but depending on what they found when they searched the building, I could have lost my job. To complete the sweep, they separated my partner and me, and we sat in the back of squad cars. I remember asking myself,

What if someone's injured?

How many people could be injured?

Did we accidentally kill someone?

Remorse is the most accurate word to describe what I was feeling. I genuinely felt that whatever happened inside the apartment was my fault because I had decided to chase after the kid. I sat with my thoughts the entire time they searched the building. Having to knock on every door on every level to go and inspect to make sure no one was harmed or deceased. It was gross darkness that surrounded that night, thinking of the sleep being interrupted with every brute knock.

With every second that inched on, I was feeling the weight of our reality. By doing our jobs, we had done something that might've cost someone their life, our badges, and the security of our households. To say I was sick to my stomach would be shortchanging the feelings lodged between my chest. Prayer and deep thinking kept me quite in the car. I had no idea whether I was going to return home with news that could shatter Camille and I's foundation. But because of grace or maybe even luck, the officers made it back and alerted that no one had been injured or killed. They said it as calmly as something you'd tell your child when giving them the good news.

The jokes began to run in about us missing out on being promoted because we didn't get shot ourselves. It was as if the night hadn't even happened as swiftly as the energy shifted after the building check.

Not for me, though.

I knew that my job wasn't lost, but my desire to be an officer was. My father had been on the force twenty-five years and hadn't had to go through something like that. My brother had been serving four years and hadn't been in the middle of a shootout. It was madness. I was doing the exact thing they'd done, yet I was getting different results. How in the hell was I supposed to reconcile almost dying before even living? I might've had post-traumatic sport disorder before that call, but I surely had post-traumatic stress disorder afterward—all for only $36,000 a year.

My life was worth $36,000 to the Chicago Police Department.

At a time when Chicago was ranked number one for homicides in the country and I patrolled the top homicide area in the entire city... realizing I hadn't lived nor could I pay for the lifestyle I desired, that shootout was the wake-up call I needed. I knew that I was done; I just wasn't finished.

MILLIONAIRE MOMENTS

Today I want you to reflect on this statement:

If I'm going to risk my life daily, by working brutal hours and maybe even in an unsafe environment, why can't I do/have more?

After taking a moment to reflect, feel free to write down your answer somewhere safe. You can even share it with me by sending me a message on Instagram: @9to5millionaire

Unfinished Business

When people ask me why I didn't quit as soon as I realized I was done with my job, I point them back to the understanding of vehicles. Once I knew my life was worth pennies to them, I started to ask questions like:

What happens to my family, my legacy and my friends if I pass away now?

What do I have to leave behind?

What would I even be remembered for?

Those questions helped me re-shift my mental framework when it came to my dreams. Remember, my intention since a young boy was to become a millionaire. But when my first vehicle got derailed, I began to fall for the American dream trap. I got a good job with benefits. I had made my family proud. I was an officer for the community I grew up in. As far as moral compasses go, mine was looking perfect. Slowly, I fell away from my dream of making big money and causing an even bigger impact.

My wake-up call triggered my mind to stop buying into the company culture and start thinking about my future dreams. But I was wise enough not to quit just because my emotions were no longer involved. I was done, but I was far from finished. This is the mindset you have to have when working a job you're not passionate about, but it works. You can't quit just because you aren't in love with your work. You have to think, strategize and re-frame your reality before moving forward. Because what's making you angry probably isn't even the job. It's the lifestyle that's dictated by a paycheck you get every two weeks. When you work hard, pour out your time, give all of yourself and you get crumbs in return; you become resentful. You begin to place your unmet desires on the back of a company that never promised you that lifestyle in the first place.

The crazy part is, people have this odd it won't be me mentality. They believe that they're resilient enough not to fold under the pressures of their job. That they're the one that's going to avoid gaining the additional weight, becoming distant family members, losing their drive for life; all the while, everyone that came before them fell for the trap. It's like being a mouse with cheese tunnel vision. Have you ever seen a mouse stuck to a sticky trap with a piece of cheese on it? They had no idea that going to get some lunch was going to be their demise. Even worse is the mouse that sees another mouse already entangled in the sticky paper, but he's so focused on the reward of the cheese that it overlooks the dangers of pursuing it.

It's a never-ending cycle of the lust of the eye versus reality. Because we all know our jobs can't sustain us alone. They weren't built to do that. Companies exist to solve problems, not pay bills. No matter how insane it sounds, the creators of these business structures weren't looking to create jobs that ensured their employees could take lavish vacations and buy expensive homes. When they built their company, they were thinking about being an industry leader and serving their customers. That means the employee, sadly, comes last.

Chapter 6

ONE STREAM ISN'T ENOUGH

When I first told Camille about the shooting, it was another reminder of how strong a woman she is. She came from a family with a strong spiritual background and was around my family for so long; that when I told her about the incident, she reminded me that God had always been my protector. She wasn't afraid of being the wife of an officer because she understood the nature of the job. I've been forever grateful because she was the sounding board I needed at a time like that.

Navigating the thoughts of doubt, concern and worry after the shootout led me to seek advice from loved ones that could relate, mainly my father. He told me to treat my job as a movie role. Every time I put on my uniform, I was to transform into a character. While on the job, I needed to be Officer King. I focused on getting the job done and making sure I made it back home. Once it was time to clock out, I needed to take my uniform off and leave the job's worries at the office. By the time I made it home, I was a husband, a son, a friend. Learning how to become a character was what had allowed my father to separate the traumatic experiences that come with the type of work we did from the peace of home. I learned how to do the same.

While speaking with other officers (including my

brother Tommie), I realized how many people suffer from some of the same thoughts.

"Is this job worth it?"

"What am I gaining by risking my life every day?"

"Is the toil of this job going to kill me?"

We gave each other our shared experiences to make sure we didn't burden our spouses. No matter how that sounds, coming home to tell your spouse about another dead body, another shootout or another burglary isn't exactly keeping the romance alive. Like most coworkers, we bonded and respected each other for the sacrifices we gave to a job that didn't sacrifice for us.

To help us heal, they gave my partner and I a week off. Those few days of separation allowed me to analyze my current situation honestly. On the surface, it was a reminder that nothing is stable, secured, nor promised. Absolutely nothing. We think we get into these companies to rise in rank to establish ourselves as beings of power, but we don't own anything in reality. As an officer for twenty years, I've served under three presidents, three mayors, and eight higher-ups. No person is really in charge. The systems are. It's the systems that govern us, not people! Do you know what stays the same no matter who comes into play? The systems we established generations before. Unless we're intentionally shifting what allows the system to run, what are we changing?

It's so dangerous to define yourself as your title. You're mayor today and a former politician tomorrow. What happens when your only successful vehicle comes to a close or an abrupt stop? Do you allow yourself to go into an identity crisis? Do you fight to be recognized by your past accomplishments? Or do you re-work your vehicles to accommodate your goals? Your vehicle is here for you. You are not here for your vehicle!

One Destination Seven Vehicles

For a moment, I'd like to revisit this idea of having multiple vehicles to get to one destination.

When I say you need multiple streams of income or multiple vehicles to accomplish your goals, I'm not saying every stream needs to be substantially different than the next. One of the most efficient ways to leverage one stream of income is to attach smaller streams to it. For example, if real estate is the overall vehicle, then each building should be attached to its own goal as a smaller vehicle. That way, the vehicle is going further than it would exist in a singular form.

Another example of having streams that coexist with each other is Toni Morrison. Ms. Morrison was an author, a professor, a novelist, an essayist, a poet, an international speaker, an editor, an activist, and more. Usually, at the same time. There's a story she shares in her documentary that details how she'd drop her sons off at school in the morning and take notes in the car while in New York traffic on a novel she was writing on her way to her job as an editor and do the same on her way to be a professor. She carved out specific times of the day to devote to writing only. All while helping the likes of Muhammad Ali and Angela Davis with their book releases. When asked about how she balanced it, she told the narrator that it was easy because she was wearing the same hat in different ways. She was an editor of books, a writer of various literary forms, a speaker, and a professor for Princeton's creative writing program. Her entire life's work surrounded one thing; using her words to tell impactful stories.

Sometimes, the streams you've been thinking so hard about are just new versions of the same stream(s) you already have access to. It won't always look like your hand being in pots of different kinds; instead, you'll notice your hand being in multiple pots of the same brand but with different functions. Being great in this way at each stream allows for the next to manifest itself.

That way, your streams are attached to your gifts, talents, skills, scope, and preferences. It doesn't have to be like this for you to find success, but it sure as hell helps you balance what's going on in your life if at least one of your streams goes back to what you do naturally. Your job, your income, and your circumstances can all change at any moment. What do you invest in that transcends time and events? What goes back to the core of who you are and what you represent?

If you can't answer that question clearly, you need to figure that out quickly. The longer you don't know what makes you stand out, you'll always be told by someone else.

Blue-Collar's Kryptonite. White-Collar's Living Water.

This kind of language isn't new for the rich. The wealthy spend hundreds of thousands on being in environments to hear the concepts being used in this book. Now I'm sure you're trying to rationalize the point of spending a mortgage note on what we like to call personal development, but it's been one of their keys to success.

I say this with love and from a place of experience; blue-collar workers tend to stay in their struggles because they think personal development is a scam or not worth the investment. The fact that you're even reading this book is monumental for these reasons.

The concept of paying for something that grows your character rather than testing for a certificate sounds foreign to the working class. Everything we do in the blue-collar world has to be attached to something tangible. We'll get a master's for the sake of a degree and an extra $10,000 to our salary, knowing we aren't passionate about the concentration.

Getting people to understand the importance of character building is hard when character isn't a skill set. So when the gap between $40,000 and making $400,000 is personal development, people's eyes roll. There are plenty of scammers waiting to eat off people's need for motivation, guidance and inspiration. But that's every industry. What company, brand or industry do you know that doesn't have bad apples?

For whatever reason, personal development is treated like an unwanted step-child in business by those who need it the most. The people that need the most inspiration are the ones that shun it. That doesn't make any sense.

Let's relate this to the example we used for multiple streams. Self-development is what keeps your vehicles' maintained. Feel like you're running low on hope, strategy, desire, passion, or even community? Attend a conference, take a course, hire a coach, sign up for a webinar, buy a book, join a book club, or enter a mastermind. Working harder doesn't get you re-inspired. New information, outlooks, and strategies do.

But if you think it's a scam, you'll never have access to the fuel that keeps your dreams going. You'll forever be the coworker complaining about their job (the same position they were praying for months prior). And come on, who wants to be that person? The person who drains everyone's souls because they decided to work somewhere while also choosing not to explore other options. If you're going to hate on the alternative methods to becoming a better person to acquire enormous wealth, keep your complaints to yourself at the least.

Blue-collar workers tend to view certain avenues as scams too. From trading currency to investing in various insurance plans, it must be too good to be true because it doesn't sound like hard work. That's why they keep choosing the same thing over and over again. The cycle of higher-education to traditional work never ends, and it rarely yields different results.

Same Day. Different Job.

Ever taken a job you didn't like just to pay the bills? I'm sure many of us have at one stage in our lives. If your purpose is strong enough, you'll learn about things you might not be the most passionate about, but you're focused on finding the vehicle that'll get you to your purpose. The hardest part for so many is that we learn the only way to earn money in this world is to work harder than everyone else. I'm not knocking hard work, but I am knocking the mindset that says it's the only way you can create an income. As you know, I'm not a fan of quitting your job; I'm pro multiple streams of revenue existing in your household every month. For most of us that aren't built like the late Toni Morrison, we have to take the time to study vehicles that we might not care about, but we're capable of using until we find our right matches.

That's the stage I was in when I realized I was over my job, but I didn't know what the next vehicle was. The first step was to figure out what I didn't know enough about and to start brainstorming what I thought I could do. But while I was igno-rant of what was next and what I needed to look into, here's what I did know.

Until that time, I had never (and still haven't) met someone who didn't complain about their job. People will brag to the world about the perks of their city job only to depress their coworkers on the clock Monday through Friday. Come Friday evening; there's the race of the weekend. The forty-eight to sixty hour time period to fit in fam-ily time, rest, grocery shopping, self-care, eating, block parties, sporting events and exercise be-fore Monday morning appears again. Blue-collar workers set up their entire weeks just to prepare for this two-day sprint. A sprint that never helps them heal from the shock placed on their bodies Monday through Friday.

I would see cops losing their bodies from drinking two cups of coffee with extra sugar and cream five times a week for twenty to thirty years. Hav-ing to smoke a cigarette every time they'd clock into work, getting four to five hours of sleep be-cause they work a part-time that's a six to eight-hour shift—killing themselves daily—destroying their relationships—all for a bi-weekly check too small to live how they want to live.

I've heard so many of my good friends and col-leagues talk about their retirement plans. It sad-dens me that there is this facade out there that someday, we will start living the best version of our life after we have enough money to retire.

Don't get me wrong; I'm not saying blow your money on silly things today. I'm telling you to do something about your income now so you can start living your best life! The retirement dream is a myth! The retirement age is sixty-seven, while life expectancy is around seventy-eight. So you're supposed to work for fifty years to enjoy eleven, maybe? Man, start enjoying life now. No one is guaranteed tomorrow. That's what I know for sure. Sidebar; but for the person that thinks you're too old to use all of this information now, know that you only believe this because you were trained to think you had to retire by a certain age. That's a limiting belief. I started speaking at forty. Your age doesn't make a difference; your choices do.

It's been my experience that people don't have not because of their age, access, education level, or because of the family they were born into; it is because of a lack of income! Ecclesiastes 10:19 says money answers all things for a reason. It's not because it's the root of life; it provides a solution for not having all the things mentioned above. At some point, we have to live our lives knowing it's not okay to be broke. Being broke is not only about not having money, but instead, missing out on having the resources to live the full experience of life.

Be real with yourself; you got comfortable, right? Listen, being comfortable is not only selfish, but it's crazy. What happens when life comes and punches you in the mouth? When an unexpected bill comes, changes occur in the economy, or you lose your job? The reality is, you don't need to spend less or get another certificate. You just need more income!

You only have to do two things differently this year than you did last year. First, learn something new each day. Two, execute on that new-found knowledge. My good friend likes to say wisdom is the application of the knowledge you acquired. If you do these two things, you can guarantee yourself a fantastic year ahead. Come up with the vision of the life you want to live, and execute. Tailor your learning to what you need to understand to fulfill your vision. Ask yourself questions like, "How much does it cost to live my dream life? How come I don't have it?" Afterward, assess your current routine.

Success has way more to do with routine than it does anything else. Things will happen in your life, but your routine will keep you on track to become the man or woman you want to be. Don't let life come and knock you down! Figure out why you've been so willing to invest more in the legacies and fortunes of families you've never met (by working their visions) than your legacy.

From Baltimore With Love

Going back to the week I had off after the shooting; my phone was being blown up with calls from loved ones checking in. Some were told I got shot (you know how word travels), while others were just seeing how I was doing mentally. I had to do a lot of story corrections, so they knew I hadn't been injured. I was happy for the love, but the best call I received came from my friend, who played in the NFL about a week after the incident. We talked about what I experienced, and his heart encouraged him to invite me out to his place in Baltimore to get my mind off of things.

There wasn't an ounce of hesitation in my voice when I told him I'd come out. I reached out to my brother and my friend Vince (who was also a police officer) to make plans immediately. I didn't have any expectations of how the trip would go either. I just knew my friend invited us out and I hadn't seen him since he started playing in the league.

The days that led up to us driving out to Baltimore were spent focusing on the reality of my current situation. I was using the time to digest that an incident like that could happen again, and it could even be worse. For the first time, I was completely taking care of myself, with this being the first significant job I ever had. At twenty-two, I kept replaying the phrase, "I just started, and I almost lost my life and my job." It might feel redundant, but I was so conflicted because this was the opposite of what I had been taught my entire life. I was raised to believe in job security, and this idea of messing that up conflicted me. Imagine how my family continually preached about this one thing, only to have it nearly jeopardized.

Despite the cognitive dissonance, I accepted job

security was an oxymoron. Anything given to you can be taken away. This was a forbidden conversation on the job and even at home. Blue-collar workers know their jobs aren't secure, but they need something to believe in so they'll continue to work. It's a process of lying to yourself to keep your sanity. They're not happy, but they pretend to be because that's the culture. And you didn't speak of these things because it would show potential weakness, a weakness that was just an awareness of your worth.

For those willing to dive into the uncharted waters of questioning blue-collar culture without bashing its foundations, exposure is the pillar to help reveal the depths of why we do certain things. Because most people say they need different, but they don't know what different looks like.

I was headed to get this exact lesson as we drove to Baltimore, and I didn't even know it.

MILLIONAIRE MOMENTS

Today I want you to reflect on this statement:

What's the facade I've created to help me cope with living a life I'm not satisfied with?

After taking a moment to reflect, feel free to write down your answer somewhere safe. You can even share it with me by sending me a message on Instagram: @9to5millionaire.

EXPOSURE

Chapter 7

THE RIDE

To show something that is usually hidden.
To tell the true facts about a person or a situation, and show them/it to be dishonest or illegal,
To let somebody find out about something by giving them an experience of it or showing them what it is like.
To put somebody/something in a place or situation where they are not protected from something harmful or unpleasant.
- Oxford Dictionary's definition of the
word exposure

There's absolutely no way to walk in truth than to be exposed to it. In the same breath, you have to be exposed to incorrect teachings and beliefs for them to be considered your own. Psychologists of various lanes have said that forty to ninety-five percent of what we do, say and feel are learned behaviors. That means your environment, your teachers and your guardians (or lack thereof), play a huge role in how you're going to make your decisions and base your beliefs. So, you are your own person, but only up to an extent.

Let's get honest with ourselves.

How often do you find yourself saying things like your parents, taking on the phrases of your closest friends or expecting the same life built by your grandparents? Matter of fact, how many times do you find yourself saying things like:

"Dang, I sound like my mama."

"I know better than to do that. My pops used to do this all the time."

It doesn't matter if you never saw someone in your family acting a certain way all the time; if you didn't get to be around them frequently, all it takes is one time to see something for you to learn it. So if the majority of these instances include people who only believed in working traditional city jobs, taking local vacations, and never discussing the importance of investing their funds, your likelihood of wanting to be different is slim. Suppose I hadn't been exposed to shows like *Lifestyles of The Rich and Famous, Cosby Show* or professional sports, who knows what I might have declared when I was eight. I more than likely would have said something along the lines of being an officer. A self-fulfilling prophecy I would fall into when I needed a backup vehicle for my dream destination. But if I didn't come from a lineage of officers, I wouldn't have even thought about being a cop as a job.

What you're exposed to dictates so much.

Often we believe we're the sole decision-makers for our lives. Meanwhile, great grandma's decisions, your neighborhood's kids, your community and your schooling, are helping you say yes or no to every opportunity that comes your way. This is the foundation of the quote, "What makes us different is what we do differently." It's the complete opposite of insanity (doing the same thing expecting a different result). Think about it; if you're old enough to know any children that you've been able to see grow up, you can trace back every major decision they've made to their circumstances. Our children watch and copy our lives and the lives of the people closest to them. We do the same as adults. I believe your level of exposure determines your level of success.

If more under-served students had access to millionaire mentors, don't you think they'd try to become one themselves? It takes a crazy amount of entitlement to expect someone to believe in something they've never seen before. That's like asking someone to want to be an astrophysicist, and they've only seen managerial positions at the plant. What you see as a child is going to shape your thinking as an adult.

The decision to stay that way comes once you're old enough to recognize your happiness, fulfillment and passions. Eventually, you'll be of age (if you're not already) to decide the kind of environments you want to try out and the types of things you want to learn. It could start as small as saying you want to visit the opposite side of your city just to see what goes on over there. As an adult, you have more say in what you can and cannot get access to. And if you've been waiting on someone to permit you to explore yourself, well here you go. You have the right to ask why you do what you do, why you believe in what you think, and what you want to learn more about.

MILLIONAIRE MOMENTS

Today I want you to reflect on these questions:

What are some habits that you and those closest to you have in common? Are they allowing space for growth or are they holding you back?

After taking a moment to reflect, feel free to write down your answer somewhere safe. You can even share it with me by sending me a message on Instagram: @9to5millionaire.

Gated Communities

It's not that you often get around people who think and act on a different level. So when my friend called me and invited me to Baltimore for a few days to get my mind off the shootout, I jumped at the opportunity. Because of how quickly I went from being a student-athlete to a graduate, to an officer, I didn't have a moment just to kick it. This was the first time in awhile I could just be Jemal. The first thing I did was talk to Camille and call up Tommie and Vince, one of my close friends and partners in the police department. I made sure I had my boys with me because I cannot stand long drives. I was never a big fan of road trips even as a kid. It was also my first time visiting Baltimore, so I had no point of reference if anything went wrong on the road.

Once I got a yes from everyone, we decided on the actual date that we'd drive to Maryland. I didn't have any real expectations of how the trip was going to go. It was my first time around NFL players in their homes and environments. I just knew we'd have a good time because of my relationship with my friend, and that I needed the break.

That upcoming Thursday had come, and we loaded up my 1993 Chevy Blazer to make the eleven-hour trek. As soon as we started the drive, the rain started pouring down. We crossed through Illinois, Indiana, Ohio, and Pennsylvania before we finally reached Maryland. Even then, the rain was coming down like a child that wouldn't stop crying. But I kid you not, as soon as we arrived at the gated community, the rain stopped, and the clouds began to part. It was literally like something straight out of a movie.

For the first time I was driving through a neighborhood where every house didn't look the same, there were different cars in every driveway, children were going to school while wearing plaid uniforms. It was like I went to an entirely new land. I immediately knew I was supposed to call this my normal.

As you can imagine, Tommie, Vince, and I were geeked! We were in awe of the neighborhood, but once we pulled up to his house, we were overly impressed. All I could think about was how much space his home took up. When my friend came outside to greet us, it was all love. I introduced him to Tommie and Vince, and we headed inside to settle in. We immediately noticed how he was a provider for his family. At the house, there were his two sisters, brother, and his mom. We watched him use the NFL to take care of his loved ones. He was one of the first people my age that I saw doing this and didn't have to do it. The NFL gave him the means to do this, and he did it with gratitude.

The first thing we did was go out to eat with his friends. The experience was wild for us. Because they were known players in the city, they got access to entering the restaurant through a secret hallway that led to the back of the establishment. Once we got there, everyone sat down and just started rattling off what they wanted to eat to the waiter. At first, I thought that they must have the menu memorized, so when it came to my turn, I asked to see one. I knew our worlds were vastly different at this point. My friend looked at me and told me I didn't need the menu because I could order whatever I wanted.

I was confused.

How could I order whatever I wanted if I didn't know what the restaurant served? My blue-collar mindset was peeking through. I didn't understand the concept of whatever you like back then. I was down to order anything as long as I knew what my options were. So I insisted on getting a menu to at least spark some ideas of what I wanted to eat and to ensure that I wasn't spending my light bill money on a T-bone steak or something. As soon as the waiter handed me the menu my eyes went directly to the right side! Now, I'm sure that I'm not the only person in the world who's done this, right? I really didn't know what I wanted to eat at that moment. I noticed how my guy and his NFL teammates knew exactly what they wanted to eat before they sat down! They never needed a menu to look at because they didn't care about prices. They just got whatever they wanted to eat! But whenever I would order, my eyes would go directly to the right side of the menu. But in reality, I was checking to see what I could afford. I know that in this example I'm talking about food, but how many of you reading this book are living on the right side of the menu of life? How many of you all are counting the cost when it comes to having the full experience of life and not solely making decisions on the cost of a thing? That's why I always say to live life on the left side of the menu! You should never be satisfied with just being in the building. It was an unusual moment because up until this point, I blended in with every other player. I had the height, the size andthe knowledge. Everyone just assumed I was a player too. But I didn't have the same mindset as them. When I got paid, I had to go into work to pick up a $1,200 check every two weeks. They got

$200,000 checks per game with incentives delivered to their homes. Our worlds were far more different than just our bank accounts.

It was the experiences, the mindsets, the expectations, the privileges, the access. I had enough money coming in to take care of Camille and I. He had enough money to take care of a child he hadn't even birthed. Family members that he didn't have to take care of. Women he didn't intend on marrying. This struck me the most. Here I was with the woman of my dreams, and I couldn't afford to give her the life she deserved. All the while, my friend was able to buy expensive bags for women he barely knew (or cared to know). It wasn't even jealousy that was consuming me as I began to compare our worlds. It was partly shame (thinking of my wife) and excitement (thinking of the possibilities).

When I wasn't psychoanalyzing our world's, we were cracking jokes and having a great time. Our entire stay was full of moments worth laughing at, and the environment was always relaxed. You could tell that there were very little life-stressors weighing them down. I had always been around people who were grateful for their jobs, but I had never been around people who were happy because of their work. There wasn't a single moment where someone said something like:

"Man, I gotta go to work tomorrow."

"I have to work overtime this week."

"Our checks are late."

They got to be their authentic selves because income wasn't an issue. They were the decision-makers. What to eat, how many cars to park out front, and what investments they wanted to make. When the four days concluded, and Tommie, Vince, and I loaded up the Chevy to head back home, I was full. It was a Monday morning when we hit the road, and my main thought was damn. "I wasn't feeling a way about missing out on the opportunity to play the sport. I was feeling a way because I saw my goal destination being lived out. I knew I needed to find another vehicle asap, or I would get stuck in the place where I was in.

Dreams Do Come True

Although I didn't fully understand what legacy truly meant, I learned that you couldn't pass down a vehicle to your children while in Baltimore. Sure, you can get your kids an interview or even create a position in your company for them, but ultimately that's second-best to what you can give them. The best thing you can pass down is a mindset of abundance and a lifestyle that reminds them that they're royalty. Now we didn't have any kids at the time, and Camille wasn't pregnant, but my mind was being trained to start thinking bigger again. I needed to pick a new vehicle to pair with my job that could run for a substantially long time.

I'm forever grateful for the twenty-two-year-old me for saying yes to this trip. I needed to experience what I read about in Rich Dad Poor Dad to make the lessons tangible. It gave the words on those pages life! I made the mental connections between my favorite shows as a kid, the first book I ever read, and this experience. I started asking:

If blue-collar workers are exposed to hard work and loyalty, why aren't we also exposed to the benefits of our labor?

Why does retirement have to be my promised land?

Has it always been like this? Have the hardest working people always had the least?

It was like I was experiencing a sort of power-up. Like the programming trying to overtake my mind all of a sudden had a system malfunction, and I was getting back to myself. I even started to assess the sort of relationships I had with those around me. Most people are, if you look at their five closest friends, around people who are like them. I realized that 99% of people aren't going to have people in their circle like my friend. That almost guarantees they're not going to get that type of exposure. I was blessed with a once in a lifetime opportunity!

Some will ask how, since he didn't offer me any money, set me up for a tryout or put me on his payroll. People that think you have to get something tangible to be presented with an opportunity don't understand how vital exposure is. Here's the deal. There's no way in the world anyone could experience something like that and go back home and not start dreaming bigger. That trip confirmed everything I wished to be true. That you can live a life where money doesn't enslave you and you can be happy while you do your work. You can be as giving as you want to be. You can experience the best parts of living while you're still young. You can get checks with at least six digits in it at a time. Us deciding to visit someone outside of our immediate circle shifted the trajectory of my life story.

Dream Bigger

Before spending four days in Baltimore, the type of leveling up I had been exposed to included being asked if I planned on becoming a sergeant or lieutenant. The level up was connected to the advancement of the company, corporation or brand. I'm sure you can relate. It always seems that achieving personal growth is tied to your position or employment. Loved ones ask when you're going to go back to school to get that $10,000 annual salary raise. They're trying to figure out when you're going to start thinking about applying for that promotion at the job you hate. After reading this far, I hope you're beginning to realize that it's not that they're ill either. They can only see as far as they've been shown. Breaking this trend is literally up to you.

The most common rejection heard when I encourage someone to step out of their comfort zone and seek new opportunities is money. Everyone says they don't have the income. I'll ask, "What's standing between you and your dream life?" The immediate response is finances. But when I ask, "What's keeping you from the finances?" very few know the answer is exposure.

Let's say you don't have a friend that plays for the NFL... then it's your responsibility to figure out how to get exposed to something similar to your ideal lifestyle. You could start by doing the following:

Ways to expose yourself so you can start dreaming bigger.

Find a neighborhood that's being built and walk through the homes.

Drive through neighborhoods that remind you of the kind of homes you want to live in.

Change who you're following online.

Take a screenshot of a bank account photo and make it your background.

Invest in more books like these.

Sign up for courses like Make Real Estate Real and connect to the internal community.

Join Facebook groups that connect you with like-minded people.

Enroll in entrepreneurship cohorts and get connected with mentors.

Once you begin to intentionally position your life in a way that welcomes new information, new access, and new people, you'll start to reap the benefits of experiencing different things. I'm telling you; exposure shapes every decision we make! No one is gifted enough to create what they can't see or haven't heard of. In some way, we're inspired by bits and pieces of what we've been able to encounter in life.

Self-Awareness Makes You Wealthy

The first question I want you to ponder is whether you're selling your time for money. In other words, is the only way you're making money dependent on you to clock-in? If so, why do you think you have for so long? When I started studying the one-percenters, I realized they were working the same, if not fewer hours, in the 9 to 5 grind. But they were earning ten times, even 100 times more. And like our former First Lady Michelle Obama said, most of these people in high positions aren't smarter than you, more skilled; they're not even more talented. They just know a few things that you don't. They understand where they came from, which bad habits held them back, where they want to go, and systems that allow them to move accordingly. That's all! They're not taking secret pills to make them more intelligent than you. They're just aware of themselves and what's going on in the world.

Chapter 8

WHAT SUCCESS FEELS LIKE

I was sick to my soul when I first got back from Baltimore. I spent all these years talking about being a millionaire. And I got slapped in the face by what that reality looked like. It didn't make me miss the game, but for the first time, I was able to see what NFL money could do up close and personal. Forget the cars, the houses, the food and all. I was stuck on what he was able to do for his family and friends without stress! Man, I was telling everybody about our experience when we got home.

It's not like I was visiting someone that I had just met. I was with my boy from Western days. We went to the same training sessions. We played on the same team. We experienced the same wins and losses. We both had NFL dreams. Shoot, even our family dynamics mirrored each other! He had two sisters, so did I. He had an older brother, so did I. We ran the race together, but he crossed the finish line. His family benefited from crossing over while mine got the pride of me assimilating to the family legacy. Seeing what he was able to do messed with me for a short while. I felt like I had fallen short, and it impacted my family.

That weekend in Baltimore was personal for me.

I meet people all the time that get access to op-portunities and miss out on the magic because they can't make it personal. They get to meet people, attend events, go to special meetings/ outings, and it's just a moment for them. They'll even watch inspiring documentaries and keep the experience outside of themselves. They don't make any moves. Some people view life from a player's point of view, while others see it as a spectator. The spectator has no clue they're play- ing the game even if they don't like it. That wasn't me. I knew if my friend could do it, I could too.

At this stage of my life, I needed a wake-up call as loud as Baltimore. My reality looked nothing like his because I wasn't doing anything like him. As an officer, it was expected of me to pick up a second job. Many don't know it, but cops have to supplement their income with a second part-time gig to bring in enough money to live comfortably. We're not allowed to get a second job while go- ing through our probationary period, but once I made it through mine, I bought into the two job system.

Because I worked midnight shifts as an officer, I decided to take on a school gig as an easy part- time job. I would work from 12 am to 8 am as a cop and then clock in at a local high school as a security guard from 9 am to 2 pm. I only last- ed two weeks at the school because I hated the work so much. While I was working various part- times, my health became compromised because of a lack of training; I was eating way more fast food because of time constraints, I barely saw Camille; I wasn't living my life the way I should've been at twenty-two. For the first time in my life, I had bought into the mindset of those around me. I intentionally wanted to fit in so I wouldn't compromise my job. It's wild because I didn't even need a part-time job. Camille and I didn't have any kids, and we were living with my parents. All we had to do was stack our money, but the additional time would have felt odd. I watched my brother and father balance two to three part-times alongside their full-time jobs. Blue-collar workers are built to believe they have to clock-in to bring in extra cash.

But where does the time go? And is it worth it? Way too much time is getting sacrificed in the current system for such a small return on investment. You break your back to pay bills. You lose your body to maintain a career. Eventually, you're either tired because you have to go to work or exhausted because you just got off.

So we run to get a promotion to try and circumvent our lack of income. But when someone gets promoted, it only changes them. Very rarely does it impact the lives of the people around them. It just helps them amass more social currency in the form of respect and a little extra money. Going from being an officer to a sergeant was enough money to get a new car, not an entirely new lifestyle. It's two times the risk but not two times the pay.

It's not even about the promotion affording you new luxuries. A job promotion isn't about the cars you drive nor the places you get to see. The stress behind getting that next promotion needs to get assessed.

Why do you want to be promoted?

Is the amount of work required in the new position worth the additional stress it'll bring?

How much money are you going to bring in every year post-tax based on the raise?

Being on a quest to build wealth isn't the problem. It's always the means of creating it that raises concern. I encourage you to look for a purpose that goes beyond yourself so you can ask how your wealth is going to (practically) help those around you. Although it makes us feel relevant and valuable, pride doesn't shift the environments of those around us. It's just clout, and unfortunately, clout can't get passed onto the next generation, nor does it pay bills.

Returning To Baltimore

Slowly but surely, I got to the point where I realized people were living just like NFL players without ever touching a football a day in their life. I was desperate to be in environments like theirs now. I knew that for my mind to take a complete 180, I needed to visit Baltimore as often as possible. More so, I needed to bring my friends and family with me so I wouldn't be the only one evolving. Driving to Baltimore became a new habit, and the trip was always worth it.

Every time I went, I brought someone with me. While we were there, I made sure we weren't moochers either. We covered our meals, travel and other expenses. Our mission was to get as much exposure as possible, not free food, parties, or whatever else. That's why we were always welcome. In two years, I went to Baltimore eight times. I never pulled up with a taker's mentality. I recognized how great the environment was, and I wanted to ensure I didn't defile it by being a liability instead of an asset, including the people that came with me.

There was a time when Vince and I went back to visit, and it reminded me of how much of a stand-up man he was. As usual, we all went out to eat with my friend's family. To be specific, we went to Dave and Buster's with all of his family in town. To add context to Vince's character, Vince represented the highest level of blue-collar. He had made it to the mental space of living in surplus. Now, Vince wasn't rich. His salary was similar to the rest of ours on the force. But during this trip, he did something that most working-class people won't. He went to the waiter and paid for the entire table's dinner and drinks without my friend knowing. When it was time for the bill, and my friend went to pay, he was pleasantly surprised to learn Vince had covered everyone. Back then, I saw it as a kind gesture. But now that I am that friend for so many, I understand why it got Vince so much respect.

People, knowingly and unknowingly, tend to be vultures. They get access to the good life attached to you, and they want to receive it as often as possible. Few people go out of their way to chip in when they believe, you got it like that. Vince took the money he earned by being an officer full-time and working at a school part-time to bless a group of people he didn't have to. That's how I know Vince had transcended to a different mindset. Blue-collar says, take care of yourself, but you can't do much for others because of their fixed income. When the bill comes, people are arguing over who ate the appetizer, what drink they drank, and who ordered the extra side of fries There's no community in finances for the working class. Maybe it's because of how hard it is to make money in the blue-collar system. So when it comes to spending it, we fight tooth and nail to ensure we're getting our exact order, the best discounts, and more.

We never messed around when we returned from our trips. I wasn't exposed to how big of a shark I was in my community until I was forced to switch environments. Every trip made us reflect on how much more there was to learn, unlearn, accept and change. The first thing I decided to get together was my mindset.

I Know Why But I Don't Know How

I genuinely had no idea how I would get the income to change the trajectory of my family's life. I just knew I had to study to show myself approved. Before these trips, I was like most people. Full of self-pity and one-day phrases. I was hoping, wishing, even praying that I wouldn't live like that forever. But I wasn't putting in any real work to force my dreams into fruition. I was just talking about a better life. I was talking like the 99% but dreaming like the 1%. There was a constant internal war that I couldn't pinpoint before I pulled up to that gated community. I mean it when I say Baltimore slapped me in the face. I could no longer brush over how much I desired to live larger than life. And the only thing that had been slowing me down was myself.

I was the one not actively looking for a new vehicle.

I was the only one making my desires a fantasy instead of a strategy.

I was the only one settling for thoughts of future wealth and bliss.

That was all me. My community didn't stop me. My wife wasn't conspiring against me. My father wasn't holding me back. Jemal was the one that wouldn't let Jemal go after his dreams. And if you ask me why I believe it's the amount of work it would take to figure it out. People don't shy away from dreams because the dream is too beautiful. They shy away because of the commitment it requires to achieve it.

Designing a new mental framework started when Camille bought me Rich Dad Poor Dad. It was a habit of hers to buy me self-help books, and this was the first one she got for me. Quickly, this book became my favorite of all time. I consumed it like it was food. I made the words personal, just like the trips. Kid you not, I felt like the author was foretelling my life story. I might've been poor dad now, but I was becoming rich dad for sure. I didn't read that book for leisure. I read it with a goal in mind. The question that roamed my mind before opening the book was, "How can I make it out?"

I started thinking about the Edward Jones licensing I acquired while I was still in the academy. I got my Series 7 and my Series 63, which allowed me to sell securities and insurance. I let it go because it felt like another job, similar to how the school gig felt. I saw that I was consistently trying other avenues, but I wasn't serious enough about them. My main goal was to figure out the next vehicle I planned on investing in with all that I had.

Prior to visiting my friend, I showed up to work like the rest of the force. I wasn't exactly a company man, but I did what was expected of me. During downtime, I did what everyone else did. We ate the donuts and would park next to each other and talk for hours. It felt like a fraternity of sorts. We all went through a rigorous initiation process, converted into becoming something like brethren, and followed each other's daily actions.

After Baltimore, I started to show up differently. Nothing on the job changed either; it was just my mental state. I noticed that outside of my mind, I had to get my time together now. How did I expect to live a different life than everyone else if

I spent my highest currency the same as them?

Time Is Greater Than Money

The most impactful takeaway from our travels was the realization of time being more excellent than money. I had been reintroduced to the idea of a routine, something I hadn't practiced since college. Things changed when I allowed myself to start living my life based on an itinerary again. Here's an example of what my schedule looked like in college.

TIME	TASK
4:00 AM	Wake-up
4:25 AM	Practice
6:30 AM	Showers
7:00 AM	Team Breakfast
8:00 AM	Classes Start
11:00 AM	Lunch
12:00 PM	Classes
2:00 PM	Football Practice
5:00 PM	Team Workout /Film
6:00 PM	Tutoring Session
7:30 PM	Team Dinner
8:30 PM	Studying and Classwork
10:30 PM	Sleep

I designated over sixteen hours of my day to a specific job as a student-athlete. Yet, as a cop, it felt like my day was a free for all. I don't even know how I thought it was reasonable for me to fall into the trap. I knew that for me to take actionable steps that led to success, I needed to base my life on an itinerary. My success would be directly tied to the amount of structure I could create in my life. Chaos has never created order. It's always been the opposite: Order tames chaos. It creates an environment for something to be created and thrive. The further we run away from order, the further we run away from efficient systems that breed success.

I credit this realization to my friend. While we were in Baltimore, he managed to keep his routine and be a hospitable host. He was still living his life on an itinerary to take care of his body and maintain a sense of normalcy. Above almost everything he valued time. Mind you, the training and recovery sessions he had scheduled in weren't mandatory for his team. He just took his career seriously enough to include extra work into his everyday life.

That's how the majority of millionaires move. Millionaires value time. Blue-collar workers kill time to make it go by faster. When you don't have a plan for what you're aiming for, you don't respect time, so you try to kill it. You do things that aren't important because you don't understand that you're required to respect it. You only kill things that are considered your enemy. When you're doing things that are taking away your joy or not adding any actual value to your life, time is something you feel like you have to fight. You wake up begging for it to be night time. You get to the evening and pray for it to hurry and become day. Specifically, so you can get to Friday evenings only to mourn Sunday nights.

WHAT SUCCESS FEELS LIKE

Creating a personalized itinerary allows you to give your time a job. The seconds in your day are just like the dollars in your account. If you don't tell them where to go, they'll find places on their own and likely get wasted. Now, even without a clear plan of how I was going to become a multi-millionaire, I had something to demystify the retirement and promotion lies. I was learning to be my conductor. That meant retirement and promotions could no longer be hung over my head as these extraordinary prizes. I was able to recognize them both as gambles. If you put everything you have into a job, you can still only make so much money there. It's the yellow brick road that leads to a lie. You were waiting on the retirement package and the promotions just to realize they weren't enough. All that time, you had the power to promote yourself. You were the only one you were waiting for.

As long as you don't conduct your own time, someone else will do it for you. Every second you don't command yourself is being mastered over by a company or working-class expectations.

To think I learned all of this by driving eleven hours outside of my community a few times a year. Exposure changed my life by showing me the fundamentals of being the conductor of my train. Here are the steps I took to lay my foundation.

#1 Decide what you want first. If you can't describe the lifestyle you desire in detail; you're headed nowhere fast. You should know the type of home you desire, the kind of family dynamic you seek, and your intended contribution to society.

#2 Get exposed to the things you want. You have to be able to hold it at some point in your life. Seeing it on Instagram will only do so much for your faith. Attending virtual conferences can only spark so much in your spirit. You need to stand in that house. Read books about the family relationships you wish to create. Go on vacation in the place you eventually want to move to. You have to make it real.

#3 Make the exposure personal. If you don't put elements of yourself into the visible picture you're creating, it'll continue to feel like it's outside of yourself. You have to feel yourself inside the experience.

#4 Internalize the feeling and take steps to make it permanent. Now that you know how you want to feel, you have to create a strategy based on turning that fleeting feeling into a permanent lifestyle for yourself.

MILLIONAIRE MOMENTS

Today I want you to reflect on this question: What does success feel like to you?

After taking a moment to reflect, feel free to write down your answer somewhere safe. You can even share it with me by sending me a message on Instagram: @9to5millionaire.

Chapter 9

YOUR LEVEL OF EXPOSURE DETERMINES YOUR LEVEL OF SUCCESS

Thinking back on my first visit to Baltimore always brings me to a place of being grateful. When we pulled up in my 1993 Chevy Blazer, I couldn't even fathom how it'd feel to live the same. I just knew what I had to. But now, it's crazy even thinking about it. I live in a similar neighborhood, in a house that's even bigger than what I saw, driving cars just as nice, and I'm able to serve my family in the same capacity that I saw my friend doing for his family.

My family literally has everything we saw and experienced on that trip times two. And we built it all while I was an officer.

I know my journey isn't conventional. It's not even expected. But I need you to remember that everything I did for my family, you can do for your own. I'm not a genius that knows all of the right decisions to make. I have to study just like you. I have to try and fail just like you. The only difference is that I'm crazy enough to keep trying! My life is the fruit of consistency, perseverance, and dedication. I was consistently trying. I persevered through the turmoil I had to face as a new entrepreneur. I was dedicated to my destination and not just the vehicles getting me there. All of those things are subjective decisions! No one can teach you how to become more consistent. Only you can make that decision for yourself.

Again, exposure is the fuel that allows you to avoid burning yourself out from all the mental work that comes along with building your dreams. Brick by brick, you're laying your foundation. And any time you feel like you don't have the strength to lay another brick down, expose yourself to something that'll remind you of what you're building, and why you're making it. I intentionally decided to visit my friend at least four times a year, for that reason. You can say it was something like once a quarter, but we would mainly go during his off-seasons because it wasn't about watching a football game for us, it was about getting exposed to a whole new world! It was a trip we took seriously. We couldn't let ourselves slip back into old habits by forgetting the things we had experienced in Baltimore. No, we knew that as long as we could hold on to the feeling we got while visiting, it would help us keep pushing forward. Even after he was traded to the Atlanta Falcons, we'd still make sure we could come out. Every time, we'd find ways to add new value too. We never wanted to feel like burdens while we were in town. We had a mission! I studied how my guy would conduct his days, and what areas did he have total control in where I needed to become more disciplined. How did he handle the pressure of his career? Did he even feel pressure? How did they handle family matters? What were the things that money solved that I wasn't even aware of? How did they protect their income? We never drove eleven hours just to kick it. I treated it the same way someone treats studying abroad or taking on an internship. I was there for class and eager to learn.

The fact that we were even able to see this as an opportunity is special. None of us were NFL players except for him. Yet, we could know we didn't have to study other successful officers. We could learn from anyone modeling the type of success we wished for ourselves. The more we studied people outside of our professions, the more insight we got on what it meant to make it out. No matter what they did to make their money, there were certain principles that they all considered valid. The most important was time. So when I understood the importance of routine again, it introduced me to the concept of The Hole.

As an officer, there are certain parts during our day that we call the hole. It means you're on duty, but there's nothing to address currently. In the beginning, we would just park next to each and talk for hours. We'd talk sports, share stories, and complain about the job. It was a moment to decompress with each other while on the job. I willingly went along with all of this up until Baltimore. But afterward, I just couldn't waste my time like that anymore. Instead of kicking it with other officers, I decided to use that time to study other streams of income, reading, and looking for Camille and I's first house, a moment that would change the course of our lives.

Seventy-Seven Visits

When Camille and I were getting ready to purchase our home, we were connected with April. She was, and still is, one of the best brokers in the game. That's why I've continued to work with her for nearly twenty years. April made sure we made the best real estate decisions for our circumstances. Initially, we were looking for a home to live the American dream and become a united family. But because of April's foresight, she knew that it would be far more beneficial for us to get an investment property first, then use the profits from it to purchase our first home. I wouldn't have even thought about doing it in that order. We were so tethered to the system of thinking back then, that investing sounded like something we should do after we got our cars and homes. April's simple advice completely shifted the trajectory of our lifestyle.

It didn't take much to convince me that she was right. I decided to take immediate action by shifting my time during the hole again. Instead of reading or working out, I started visiting rental properties. And I wasn't looking based on my feelings either. I had a set goal in mind. We knew the home that we wanted to purchase would have a $1,500 house note every month. So any property that couldn't profit a minimum of $1,500 was an immediate no. Someone else might've taken the property that would've brought a profit of $1000 every month. To be frank, that's not even a bad deal. But we knew what we were looking for and didn't plan on stopping until our entire checklist was checked off.

Every single day, I was looking at different properties. Going in to evaluate them myself, learning what was considered good and bad. Eventually, I became a king for assessing property because I was physically visiting locations. And after visiting seventy-seven different buildings in less than two months, we finally decided on our first investment property. Yes, you read that right. In less than sixty days, I took myself to seventy-seven different buildings to assess while working my job. I hope talking to you about the hole didn't make you think we weren't working the majority of our shifts. Crime doesn't wait on convenience. But any moment I could get to another property in Chicago, I left. No questions. I wasn't trying to wait an entire year before getting started. I already had a broker that I trusted. She introduced me to an attorney, and the attorney introduced me to an accountant. Then I got connected with a contractor, and he helped me understand construction. It was as if the right people were popping up every time I took another step of action. Mainly, the people who were working for me helped me understand the real estate game. I was so focused on the end goal that I was trying to learn from them all. I didn't care about being right. I wanted to be paid. So that meant learning from people about a new skill set and hearkening to their wisdom.

Here's how badly Camille and I wanted this:

The shootout happened in August. We had our first rental property in October! We weren't waiting on anything to change at the force. Visiting Baltimore was all I needed to realize I had to wake up. The investment property we got immediately started making us a profit. We got the four-unit apartment building for $125,000. We put $2,100 down for the security deposit to acquire it. We put $25,000 up for building renovations (the bank gave us the money for the upgrades). Next, we hosted an open house and filled the units with tenants. Each unit brought in around $1,050 a month. We averaged a little over $4,000 per month pre-expenses—all on a cop's salary.

Our system worked so well that we decided to leverage the money the property was making. Specifically, to pour it back into the building and buy our second investment property. We refinanced the first building, pulled an $80,000 line of credit, continued to save the money we were netting, and got ready to purchase our second property—all before I had turned twenty-three.

Setbacks Are Set-Ups

When we finally got our second building, we got a taste of how cruel the world can be. We had done everything according to the book, minded our business, and everything else. Still, misfortune found its way to us. In the middle of our second property rehab someone broke in and stole all of the copper piping and materials. Because I was new to real estate investing, I didn't have the right type of insurance policy which covered vandalism and theft. But Vince being the friend he was, saw how important this property was for our future and my confidence. He decided to take a risk on us that would cost him dollars and earn him an even greater respect.

That one moment of Vince fronting me the money to keep pushing was a reminder to stay focused. So we did.

After a little time and intentional saving, Camille and I started looking for our third property that would be our official home. The difference between the picturesque homes we were looking at and the expansive ones we could scout now was astronomical. By only using my police salary, we were looking for homes that were 900 to 1000 square feet. But using the money we were netting from our properties, we were visiting homes that were 4000 square feet on average. That's over four times the size! Our season of sacrifice paid off in a way we didn't think would be possible in our twenties. Our commitment to getting the properties changed our life *quickly*. The reason I keep writing we is because I wasn't in the trenches alone. Camille was working as an assistant manager at Enterprise Rent-a-Car, which was a job that she got right out of college. She was the youngest assistant manager in the state! On a consistent basis she would give me her entire check, sacrificing shopping and weekly beauty treatments, and didn't care about sharing that '93 Chevy Blazer with me.

I can remember family members and friends looking at her crazy for being okay with not being done up all the time. People knew we had properties and misinterpreted it as us balling. Not to knock the income we were bringing in collectively, but it wasn't even a tenth of what I dreamed about at eight-years-old. Her trust in me wasn't blind, though. She had watched me take all of my goals seriously since we were in high school. I had proven to her that my vision was worth trusting in. We moved as a team; something I know helped me press forward during low moments. Both of us refrained from going out frequently, spending money on a whim, and anything else that could've stopped us from meeting our savings goals. We knew that if we could grind while we were young, we could spend the rest of our lives having a great time together. This was before the conferences. Before having a network of solid people. Before ETA. It was just her and I working together to build our dreams.

Leverage Your Assets

Once I got a taste of what real estate could do when you added purpose to every property, I knew we had struck gold. So many people let their feelings dictate their purchasing decisions. I finally found a vehicle that could get us to our destination faster!

Does this feel like the home for me?

Do I like this property?

An extra $900 does sound nice every month.

I never wanted to make a decision that big based on how I felt. I didn't need intuition as a beginner. I needed facts and numbers that made sense. With the first building, we used my income (and some of Camille's) to purchase an income-generating asset. That way, my job could buy assets, and those assets could cover our liabilities. To keep it simple, an asset brings in money, while a liability is something that'll cost you. If you do what the average person does, you'll let your job cover your liabilities. The issue with forcing your job to simply pay your bills is you'll always have a debt to pay for. But you won't always want to work. It'll create a never-ending cycle of money coming in only to be lost to your mortgage/rent, electricity bill, daycare and other liabilities. The income from your job was meant to purchase income-producing assets, then let those assets work for you to cover your liabilities! It's the quickest way to get out of the rat race.

You don't have to be a millionaire to make decisions like this one. You just have to leverage your job to acquire assets. Then take the profits from your assets to cover your bills. That's what we did when we got our property. I like to say that we bought a building for every bill that we had and would have!

Officer salary ▸ 1st investment property ▸ 2nd investment property ▸ 1st home

You have to work your job to get as many income-producing assets as possible. My officer's salary never paid for our house bills. Our properties did that for us. All we had to do was know what we wanted so we could move accordingly.

The investments I had at the time included being an officer, real estate, and stocks. I took the knowledge I got from getting my securities and insurance certificates and learned how to invest. The profits I made from stocks were used to pour back into our buildings. I remember the first company I invested in was Krispy Kreme. It was at a time that the company was new, and it ended up being a lucrative investment. The tip to invest in the company came from Camille listening to a few top managers at Enterprise discussing how Krispy Kreme would be going public soon. I had three significant streams with mini-streams inside of them, allowing me to amass wealth exponentially.

A Million By Twenty-Six

I didn't change anything about my process in the beginning. We stuck to what we knew until we decided it was time to open up a business, specifically a line of childcare centers. It was in 2006 that we started considering getting a bank loan to get the business started. I knew it was going to be an easy process, so I decided to go to the bank that was right across the street from the police station. When I called to see what I needed to bring, they introduced me to the term portfolio, pretty much a folder that detailed every asset we had plus our liabilities. I called April to help me put the value of the assets together, and once we completed it, I took a visit to the bank. I arrived at LaSalle Bank (now known as Bank of America) soon as I got off work, which was as soon as they opened in the morning, in my old police uniform, rundown police shoes and stepped into Darrell Tucker's office.

I sat down, wanting to get a business loan, tired from working a full-shift, eyes heavy from the job but full of hope for the conversation with Mr. Tucker. The entire conversation he referred to me as Officer King. He was taking his time reading through the portfolio I had presented. He would take moments where'd he go from looking at the document to looking at me. He did this a few times before He said, "Mr. King..." Now notice the change in title. I went from Officer to Mister. I knew that something was either really great or really wrong.

He completed his sentence by saying, "Mr. King, you're a millionaire!" I looked at him, stunned. I had just turned twenty-six, and I had just clocked out of my morning shift on the job. Nothing about me looked like a million dollars. Yet, my net worth had equated to $1.6 million. I will never forget that day. I had mud on my shoes, my uniform was dirty, and I was tired from being a full-time work-er, and an entrepreneur, and a husband. I remem-ber replying by saying, "I'm a millionaire? I am?" Now mind you, this is what I wanted. I've been dreaming about this for eighteen years. To think it would manifest itself before thirty, without NFL money, wasn't something someone would expect out of a Black man from Chicago with blue-collar roots. But I always had a feeling that it was supposed to be me. From the Lifestyle of The Rich and Famous to Ducktales, I figured once I hit millionaire status, I'd be swimming in gold.

He proceeded to teach me about net worth. The definition is your assets minus your liabilities. After he finished calculating my portfolio, he said, "Mr. King, you have a $1.6 million net worth." I couldn't believe it because I was still a man in uniform.

The crazy part, I still got denied the loan because we had no experience in daycares—go figure. They argued that I couldn't get a loan without any relevant business experience. My rebuttal was that I couldn't get the experience without the loan. But instead of begging, I went back to what I knew how to do best. I started buying up properties, fixing them up, and selling them. Every time we'd sell a property, we'd use 50% to go towards renovating the daycare and 50% towards reinvesting in properties. We trusted our process to work in our favor.

The greatest part about learning about my first million was that I wasn't chasing it. I couldn't even tell you my net worth at twenty-four or twenty-five. I was so focused on purchasing assets that I had reached an eighteen-year-old goal without even knowing it. Once I learned how they calculated net worth, that's when I got strategic with my plans. At first, I just wanted a building for every bill. But now I understood this country's system, and I planned on utilizing it to the fullest. I knew that the average millionaire had seven streams of income, so I didn't plan on stopping until I had seven outside of my job! Every building and stock counted as one, and eventually, the daycare became a major source of income. I'll share that story in the upcoming chapter, though. The main point is the level of focus I had.

Even while discussing it with my parents, they weren't worried about my decisions or new ventures. They knew, "Jemal was just being Jemal." I count this as a blessing because I meet people who come from families trying to hate on their aspirations. We were blue-collar, but we weren't the kind of family to try and down one another. Our parents meant what they said when they encouraged us to be whatever we wanted as long as we committed.

The hardest part was keeping my mind in shape. That's why the next pillar of this book is all about decision making. Some people consider it fluff, but I know it's an essential thing to study. Our minds and how we decide are the most excellent tools ever created. But like every tool, we have to learn how to use it efficiently, especially when you're dreaming larger than you've ever experienced.

The culmination of having a wife that believed in me, a background that encouraged relentless work, and a drive that wouldn't allow me to settle for second-best, brought me into millionaire status within four short, but focused years. And if you ask me if I genuinely believe you can do the same, my answer will always be a resounding yes!

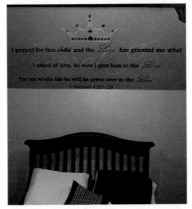

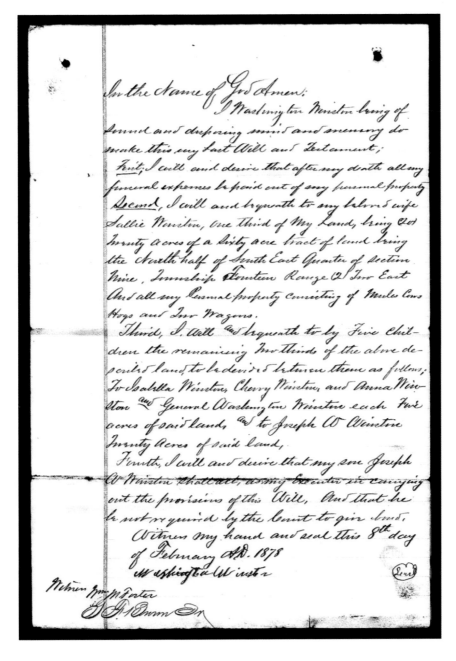

My Letter To God - Part 1

HEAVENLY FATHER, I love you!
I THANK you! AND MOSTLY, I NEED you!
THROUGHOUT MY life you HAVE ALWAYS Showed
Yourself AS THEE CONSTANT PRESENCE IN MY
life THAT HAs ORDERED MY STEPS throughout
THIS PATH OF life. lord I'm writing This love
letter to you TO ASK you FOR one OF the Greatest
Gifts That Anyone Could ever bless me with
and that Gift is Blessing me with a Son.
lord I THANK you FOR The Two Daughters th't
you have given me! I Don'T Know where or
How my life would be without Them.

My Letter To God - Part 2

They have Been the Peace and Joy of My life! lord I Thank you For The wife you have Blessed Me with! She Has Been A Angel Sent From Heaven, Hand Picked For Me From you lord and I THANK you! But Now More Than ever I want To See How it Feels to have a Son THAT Bears My name And Bears My looks And Most of all, THAT Bears The Same Faith And love I Have For you!!!

God I Beg of you To Bring Him Forth Right NOW! Bring Forth Jeral Joseph King Right now and Open The Flood Gates of Heaven and Have your Angels Deliver Him into The Belly of my wife The Same way you Blessed ME with All of The other Blessings you Bestowed on ME Throughout my life!

Lord As Always I Have Total Complete Faith in you and your word And I Know That The only Reason That MY Son is Not Here Right NOW is Cause of A lack of MY Faith And NOT of you!

So Lord Please TAKE THE GRAIN OF FAITH THAT WE HAVE AND TURN IT INTO THE HARVEST NECESSARY TO BRING Jamaker. FORTH Right NOW THIS MONTH! Im going to end this letter the Same Way I STARTED it. Heavenly FATHER I love you! I THANK you! AND Mostly I NEED you!!!

ITS ALREADY DONE!

DECISION MAKING

Chapter 10

RIGHT SIDE OF THE MENU

There's a saying that goes, "Your thoughts lead to your words. Your words lead to your actions. Your actions lead to your destiny." When I focus on the transition between an idea and the future, I reflect on the importance of decision making. It's not that we automatically manifest every thought that pops into our heads. Instead, the thoughts we allow to turn into words and actions lead to manifestation. It's like being at a restaurant, and someone asks whether or not you want soda or water. Before you give your final answer verbally, you mentally decide which was the best at the moment. You took action upon sipping from the glass. Depending on how often you choose one over the other is a reflection of your long-term health. Another example includes being given a once in a lifetime opportunity. Let's say someone presents an option for you to make the most money you've ever made, work the least hours you've ever worked, and you get to be with your family more often. Several thoughts could swarm your mind. Thoughts that tell you to hop on the opportunity immediately, or thoughts that make you question your capabilities and the fear of messing it up. The thoughts that you allow to manifest into your words will be the thought that mostly influences your decisions, thus your actions. For some of you reading this, you can't even imagine letting yourself miss out on making more money, working less, and seeing your family more. But some of you struggle with making sound decisions because of fear, sometimes even bad programming. By that, I mean the environment you were raised in, the belief systems that surround(ed) you, and anything else that influences the way you view the world and yourself.

Truthfully, I think more people struggle with the latter. I meet so many people that just can't make a decision that's best for them because of whatever reason at the time. For today's lesson, I want to focus on the idea of "affordability versus best. Without knowing it, you've probably struggled with this pillar; I know I did in my early twenties.

Affordable definition:
Inexpensive; reasonably priced.

Best definition:
Of the most excellent, effective, or desirable type or quality. To the highest degree; most; outstanding. Outwit or get the better of (someone).

Starting with the definitions, we can see that affordability doesn't encompass quality. It's only the cost associated with something that's considered inexpensive. In other words, it's accessible to the masses. On the other hand, best is predicated on the quality of something. It uses words like excellent, desirable, and outstanding. Cost isn't associated with this term due to it being about the status of a thing/person/event. I don't find it ironic that price isn't anywhere connected to the definition of best.

Here's the concept I want you to think about while reading: When money is scarce, we tend to make decisions driven by affordability rather than what's best. For example, when you're penny-pinching, you're more likely to settle for sending your child to the worst school in the district instead of picking what's best for them and creating a strategy for that decision. Internally you're at war because you're aware of the best option, but money becomes your master, and it tells you what you can and cannot do with it. You were created to subdue the earth and be the master (or good steward) of your income. So not only is making the affordable decision over the best decision hurting your lifestyle; it's also taking you out of your earthly function. As a man or a woman, you were created to rule over your possessions, not the other way around. To give more context, I'll share a story of a time that I felt most conflicted with this tug of war.

The Most Expensive Meal of All

Remember when I told you about the time we went out to eat in Baltimore? Alright, so this story is centered during our first night in town. We all went out to eat a restaurant known for expensive meals (Tommie, Vince, and I weren't aware of this fact just yet). When we arrived at the place, we went to a room in the back of the establishment, where professional players, political figures, and celebrities would eat for their privacy. I hadn't experienced anything like this! We walked in, and everyone was familiar with each other, including the players and the staff. And not because someone had a friend or a cousin that worked at the restaurant. But they had gone so frequently that eating there was just another common experience.

The part that baffled me the most was watching them rattle off what they wanted to eat before we were even seated. It was like watching a food cypher happen in front of your eyes. Guys were just yelling out requests like, "Get me a steak with a side of crab and some risotto." or "Get me an order of bourbon-glazed salmon with a side of truffles and broccolini." So when I heard, "Aye 'Mal, what are you getting?" I was confused. I assumed they had gone so often that they had the menu memorized, so I requested a copy to review for myself. My friend looked at me and said I didn't need to do that. I just needed to let them know what I wanted to eat, and they'd make it.

Now, this didn't make any sense to me. How was I supposed to tell them what I wanted if I wasn't aware of what they offer? Was this a seafood place? A steakhouse? Were they known for their chicken? I insisted on getting a menu to at least get an idea of what they sold. Little did I know that the menu wouldn't have helped my anxiety at this moment; if anything, it heightened it. My eyes started looking at the menu, and I immediately checked the right side of the menu. You know exactly what I mean too. Before checking to see the food options, I looked to see how much the food was going to cost me. The figures felt like they were burning through my skull as I stared at them.

Who needs a $200 piece of steak?

Why does this chicken cost as much as my electric bill?

I know we could've gone somewhere with food just as good and affordable.

I was in shock, discomfort, and dang near agony at the same time. I couldn't fathom spending this much on food my body was going to digest within the next hour. More importantly, I couldn't imagine spending bill money on a chicken breast. I was in the middle of saving for our first property, budgeting for bills, and trying to be prepared for miscellaneous expenses. At that time, I didn't care about the experience, my health, the recommendations they were giving me, or anything else for that matter. It was only day one, and we had three more days to ration funds. I was dreaming about a 99¢ burger or some wings that would've cost $3.99. I was also thinking of what I was going to tell Camille when I got back to Chicago. But we were there, and I wasn't about to make us go somewhere else for food, and this was also the world pre-Grubhub.

To make my decision, I found the five cheapest items on the menu and selected what my dollar could handle. Every meal was too expensive for my account, so I had to decide on what would cause the smallest blow to our finances. After picking my five items, I decided on the chicken breast meal. It took me more than ten-minutes to come to a conclusion. My heart was beating so fast I wouldn't have been surprised if I looked like one of those characters whose heart beats out-side of their chests. All this anxiety was building, and this was only my dinner. I didn't even want to order a drink or an appetizer, and I definitely wasn't even looking at the desserts. I was pro-cessing every dollar that was being withdrawn from my account to eat out with my friend and his friends. My blue-collar mentality was looking at how many hours of work this one meal would equate to.

I can't even remember the conversations held that night. I was so preoccupied with my thoughts that everything else was lost. If you asked me how I rated my food, I wouldn't have had an an-swer. Guilt had poured itself on to my taste buds and my veins. There wasn't anything enjoyable about that night. I was so tethered to money that I had let an expensive meal mess up a night that should have been one for the books. Some might wonder why I wasn't just honest with my friend and asked him to cover my meal, but I've never been that guy. I don't want to eat off of other people. Especially knowing how much a dollar costs. The sacrifice of time, physicality and mental strength add up when calculating how much a single dollar is genuinely worth. I also don't want to be known as the man that requires other men to take care of him. That never has and will never sit right with me. Even with that meal being a significant sacrifice, asking my friend to cover my plate last-minute sounded ludicrous.

After what was probably two hours, the bill appeared as a long receipt (almost as long as a Walmart receipt). The guys just started pulling out cash and putting it on the table. No one asked to fact-check, divide it up, see who ate which appetizer, or drink. They just took out hundreds of dollars and sat it on the table to chip in. Tommie, Vince, and I did the same, but not as enthusiastically as the rest of the table. Visualizing myself at that instant, I was getting a lesson on living my life based on what was affordable versus what was best, and it was a hard lesson to live through.

I remember wanting to try different dishes, but the prices handicapped my options. It was also an internal fight because I grew up eating meals like this on special occasions. That day wasn't a birthday, an anniversary, a celebratory time, nor a holiday; it was just a Thursday evening. I couldn't even think of what my father would have done after seeing the menu. My brother and I just looked at each other in disbelief. It genuinely felt like we were wasteful and irresponsible. I remember thinking, "It doesn't even take all this."

Growing up, we learned to associate best with affordability. The cheaper the meal, the better. Not because of quality, but because of accessibility. It was like we were getting the best of a company when we could get an entire meal for $5. You felt like you were stealing!

"Oh man, I got this eight-piece wing, a fry, and a drink for $5.00"

"I got a burger, a large fry, and large tea for less than $6.00!"

The catch was we were the ones getting clowned by these major corporations. They were (and still are) injecting our foods with synthetics to pre-serve shelf-lives, using the lowest-grade of meat selections, sacrificing safety standards during product-creation, and more. Yet, we thought we were the winners.

Making choices based on the right side of the menu isn't solely about your health either. It's an overall lifestyle crutch. If we live our lives letting money dictate our health status, what else are we allowing it to have dominion over? Whether we like it or not, our lives are the total of our de-cisions. I can recall this being our normal my en-tire life as a child. We'd only go to restaurants that offered *buy two, get one free* deals like TGIF. Every decision we made was about affordabil-ity. When we'd visit the baseball park, we never ordered the double cheeseburgers or the pizza slices. We stuck to the value meal that came with popcorn, a hotdog, and a small drink. Somehow living a life predicated on deals made us feel like we were one-upping society. As if we were the mature and responsible citizens, while the fans ordering the double cheeseburgers were wasteful, irresponsible, and out of their minds. Some things we hear in the blue-collar world are:

Why would I pay them for that when I can make it at home?

I could buy a whole rack of ribs for that price and cook it myself.

Why would I hire someone to fix the plumbing? I have the tools right here.

You spent how much on a new car? You should've got a cash car. They do the same thing.

I'm not spending $1,000 every month on my child to go to school. They're learning the same thing at the local public school.

You should've shopped around before going to them. I heard the outlet got it for cheaper.

You're better than me. I wouldn't have spent that much money on something like that.

If the price tag wasn't on sale or discounted, it was considered overpriced and out of reach. That's why I went into a mental overdrive when we were ordering our food in Baltimore. The voices from my parents, our neighborhood, and my colleagues were ringing in my ears. Each voice was condemning me for the purchase of a meal cooked with some of the best quality ingredients I had ever experienced. Coming out of this moment showed me how much my family and I were missing out on in the world. And I never wanted to cheat them from experiencing life to the fullest (even if it wasn't my job to provide it for them as their son or brother). Technically, Camille was the only one I had to provide for. That didn't stop me from feeling the weight on my shoulders as I finished my plate that night.

Strategizing Best Over Affordability

If you're reading this and questioning whether I'm telling you to start going to expensive restaurants and spending money you don't have, trust me when I say I'm not. I don't believe in keeping up with the Joneses. First off, the Joneses are living on credit themselves. Secondly, the Joneses aren't going to pay off your debts after you rack them up. What I'm saying is you have to become aware of why you're making the decision that you are. When you purchase something, are you analyzing the cost over the quality or vice versa? Never forget that you have to think like a millionaire before you become one.

Thoughts ▸ *Words* ▸ *Actions* ▸ *Destiny*

When you choose what university you're going to attend, are you asking how much the tuition is before checking if their program is accredited? When you decide to date someone new, are you asking how accessible they are over if their characteristics represent the best things you need in a mate? How about your first home? Are you, or did you, put location and pricing over your desire to live somewhere that would look like your ideal abode? Ask yourself about the last five decisions you had to make. What was the driving factor that led to your final decision? What was the outcome of each?

As long as you don't have a financial strategy, you'll always be forced to live like a slave to money. Every day you wake up, money will tell you how long you have to work that day, what you can eat on your lunch break, when and where you can vacation, if you can take the weekend off, what BS you have to put up with from supervisors and so on. Forcing yourself to handle this doesn't make you more down to earth, nor does it allow you to be a stronger person. If anything, money ruling your life is making you weaker. Your health and your mental state are the prime targets of its attack on your life. If it can keep you from being in tip-top shape, you'll continue to act as a consumer instead of a producer.

The key to breaking this continual cycle of making money just to stress about losing it is to have multiple streams of income. In the last chapter, we covered exposure and the impact of it. Right now, we're bringing everything you've learned thus far into remembrance. You want to make better decisions? Create an income that allows you to do so. An income that isn't based on the number of hours you have to show up physically. A system that'll allow you to make the most amount of money based on the resources you currently have at your disposal. It doesn't matter how you feel about money. Establishing wealth matters because it provides options that allow you to live a better lifestyle. By now, we know that working a 9 to 5 will never give you enough! You need outside investments to help take your lifestyle to the next level.

At birth, we get exposed to how 99% of the population lives! During our primary years, we learn how 99% of the population thinks! As adults, we work our 9 to 5's every day and get paid the same as 99% of the 99 percenters! Are we expected to live the American dream by working thirty to forty years for companies mostly owned by one-percenters all with the hopes and dreams of one day retiring as a senior citizen and finally getting the chance to live life like the 1%? The reason why it's called the American dream is that it's not real! Family, I need you to stop praying for the American dream and wake up and realize that the American dream is not your dream! The only dream you should be envisioning is the one you're creating yourself. Not the one you got exposed to, taught about, and engrained in. The vision you see when you close your eyes and think about the things you wish were true in your day-to-day.

Not once have I encouraged you to make money your life's mission. I just know you can't accomplish that mission without it. When I hear naysayers say, "Money doesn't buy happiness;" I always rebuttal with, "But it buys everything that does." That's why you can shift your mindset to a space that recognizes how vital money is without making it your chief obsession. Please understand, I don't love money. I never have, and I never will. I love the purpose behind what I'm using it for. I love sending my kids to the best schools, seeing my wife not being forced to work, watching my parents experience out of this world vacations, and everything else it allows us to do. You have to separate the love for money and the love for purpose. The money isn't anything more than a tool.

If you make money your chief obsession, you'll be devastated when you lose it. Notice I didn't say if. When you're investing in yourself, there's always the risk of losing some money. That's just a part of the cards you're dealt with. You can avoid the emotional turmoil if you're not emotionally tethered to the dollar itself. I often tell my Make Real Estate Real students: Have a purpose for every property you purchase. You should never fall in love with the property itself. You fall in love with the meaning behind the property. That goes for every income-generating asset you acquire. The purpose behind your purchase is more significant than any problem that you'll have. We're changing lifestyles, and we're changing lives. It's never been about the properties. I'm creating a legacy by making decisions centered around doing what's best for my family's longevity.

That's why Camille and I didn't become self-consumed when we found out we were millionaires. When I first told her about our $1.6 million net worth, it was business as usual. Of course, we were excited, but it felt different than what we expected. The way people talk about becoming a millionaire sounds like the government is going to send you some plaque of achievement. The words would say, "Welcome to the club! You're officially a millionaire!" But we were residing in our 4,000 square foot greystone, living a very upper-middle-class lifestyle. We were making decisions focused on where we wanted to go versus what we should be doing—and it had gotten us this far. All our millionaire status had done was confirm the importance of paying attention to those small everyday decisions.

What should we do with this check?

How can we avoid going out to eat this week?

Let's use 30% of this extra money for a small renovation in one of our units.

Receiving the coveted title of millionaire put money into even more perspective for us. It gave me access to more capital to do more things that could make more money. It got to the point we weren't talking about ideas; we were aggressively accomplishing things because we had more access. There literally weren't any more excuses. The only change was the types of decisions that we had to make.

At twenty-six, I made $52,000 a year as an officer, and I was the wealthiest person on the job (from my outside investments), but I was still dreaming. I was envisioning:

My children going to the best schools possible.
Having multiple retirement accounts.
Being able to take care of my parents and siblings by starting businesses with them.
Traveling the world.
A 10,000 square foot home.

I was living better than the way I grew up, but I wasn't near Baltimore yet. I could see the progress in route to our destination. The climate was getting warmer, but I wasn't satisfied yet. I was at the beginning. We had to decide: how many units we needed, how much money did we have to bring in from each, which stocks we were going to invest in, what kind of savings accounts were we going to open, how much we were going to invest in life insurance every month, if we were going to hire a financial planner and who we could trust with our numbers. The thing that prepared us for major decisions like these were the smaller decisions we had to make along the way.

If Camille and I couldn't: manage whether or not investing in our health was worth it, if we should get a rental property before our first home, how much we wanted to profit every month, who we needed to stop hanging with, what we were willing to sacrifice, and every other decision we were blessed to make; there's no way we would have been able to make wise decisions later.

He that is faithful in that which is least is faithful also in much: and he that is unjust in the least is unjust also in much.
Luke 16:10

Being faithful to what you have now will propel you to keep what you gain tomorrow. Even if you're not a master of this now, you can train your mind to become one. During this season of my life, I consumed a lot of motivational content. It felt like I was listening to Les Brown every day. I was also reading books like:

Cash Flow Quadrant by Robert Kiyosaki
Think and Grow Rich by Napoleon Hill
The Richest Man in Babylon by George Clason

Becoming better at being aware of your decision-making skills is determined by the amount of mindset work you put in. You can't make poor decisions for forty years and think that you will automatically do better because you decided to do better. You have to feed yourself new information that tests old habits and theories. It's your job to care enough about being an effective decision-maker. Transform yourself into an avid learner and watch your self-awareness heighten, and your decisions become more sound.

MILLIONAIRE MOMENTS

Today I want you to reflect on these questions:

Where would you be if you made decisions based on the best outcome instead of affordability for the last five years? How can you begin to work on your ability to make better decisions? Who can keep you accountable?

After taking a moment to reflect, feel free to write down your answer somewhere safe. You can even share it with me by sending me a message on Instagram: @9to5millionaire.

Chapter 11

THE MEAT WAGON

Time is the most invaluable resource you have. I cannot emphasize this enough. You think it's your money, intelligence or network. I'm here to knock all of that out of your mind. Time.. That's what you need when your back is against the wall, when you need to make a decision, and everything else. The way you utilize it is a clear representation of who you are, what you believe in, and where you're heading. I can see whether or not you're serious about your life based on the time log of your daily life. When no one's watching, what are you doing? Who are you speaking to? What are you getting done? The use of time measures a man because the use of time is made up of actions the man makes. There's no way to get around this either. You're either treating your time with the utmost respect or playing yourself, your future, and your legacy. So use it to invest in yourself! Don't wait on another permission slip to start adding value to your own life. It's your life, after all. And when you find a way to do this, make sure it doesn't require your physical body to collect the check.

I know most blue-collar workers revert to the second job mentality when we talk about doing more and self-investment. But that's the complete opposite of what I did to become a millionaire before thirty. A second job requires you to be at an establishment, either in-person or online. But investing in yourself means that you're finding a way to generate income by doing the least amount of work possible. Life isn't a game of who works the hardest. It's a game of who works the least and makes the most. It doesn't matter how you feel about it, either. That's the truth about the way this country operates. If you think about it though, it makes sense. I can't give my family financial freedom if I lose my freedom. What do I give them if I'm working eighty to ninety hours a week to bring in a small surplus of money? There's a mindset difference. The wealthy see freedom as a time surplus, not a cash surplus. When you think money is the ultimate representation of freedom, you'll always feel like you're in a cage when you lose it. You won't even be concerned about efficiently managing your time because you're chasing a couple Benjamin Franklins. Think, when you want to make more money, you more than likely resort to finding ways to clock-in instead of looking for something to study.

As a human, I know you're brilliant. I don't care about your IQ, your EQ, your credit score, your SAT, nor your GPA. Because you have a brain, a multitude of experiences, and a personality, you can think of solutions all the time. When there's no food in the refrigerator, you pull a meal together. When your kids ask you for a fun night out, you create a wonderland out of what you have. You're never short of solutions, in particular when they involve the ones you love. Yet, when it comes to yourself, you forget that you're the best guru you've ever met. You can listen to me or any other speaker, but if you don't make the decision that's the best for you, all the advice we give is pointless. We don't know your weaknesses, your shortcomings, or your failures. You do. We don't know your goals, your dreams, or your visions. That's all inside your head. Thus, I can't tell you what you need to be doing for every hour of the day. You need to take the responsibility of learning how to manage your own time effectively.

Even when you think about my earlier years, I didn't start relaxing because Camille and I learned we were millionaires. We weren't where we wanted compared to Baltimore, and I still didn't have enough resources to change the lives of those around me. If anything, I was actively looking for ways to use my time as a millionaire better. I've been doing the same thing ever since. I know that if I focus my mind on what I want my life and time to look like within the next ten years, I would've prepared myself for the coming time. Twenty-year-old me prepared thirty-year-old me. Thirty-year-old-me prepared forty-year-old-me. Now, I'm making the fifty-year-old me, and this is how I took control of my future! That's why I always say that you have to do it for the future you! So if you're going to age regardless, you should be aging as effectively as possible. Those random pockets of time slots shouldn't be random at all. They should be designed around your goals for the year, month, week and day. So as an officer working patrol and already taking great care of my time, I didn't think I could get any more blessed in terms of extra time in my day.

That was before I joined the meat wagon.

Not So Ideal Blessings

It's crazy because back in the day, the meat wagon was a position for a lot of old-timers. Cops trying to get promoted, make the arrests and use their guns, weren't trying to be caught in the meat wagon position. It was for officers that weren't trying to work hard all day. They had already been working the force for years and wanted to lighten things on up. They had no desire to answer any more calls or chase after people for old-times sake. It was pretty much seen as the lazy man's position for an overweight cop. All you did was pick up dead bodies and transport them or transport prisoners from one place to the next. You can imagine how unfavorable the position would've been amongst younger cops. We were expected to chase, apprehend, and solidify the arrests. The only time you'd see the patrol officers and the meat wagoners working together was when we needed someone to pick up the people we couldn't fit into our squad car. Let's say we arrested seven people; we'd call the paddy wagon to transport the other three people. Most of the time, they wouldn't even get out of the car to seat them inside. They'd ask if we already did our pat-downs then let us put them inside the truck before taking them to lock up.

In our world, there wasn't anything pleasant about the police van, aka meat wagon. We were raised to go after the jobs that came with the most work, the best titles, the highest pay possible, and honor. For a twenty-something, there wasn't anything honorable about being associated with a position that made you seem lazy. For that reason, it wasn't ideal to anyone outside of the old-timers, and of course, me. I knew that ideal is a personal decision. What's suitable for my lifestyle and goals might not be ideal for yours. I've never cared about acquiring honor by doing what everyone expected out of me. So when I got the opportunity to be the third man on the wagon, I was cool with it. It was meant to be a temporary solution because one of the police van guys couldn't come into work one day. As a patrol officer, we could ride in our cars alone; we called it riding 99. But because of the nature of the meat wagon, there always had to be two officers together (which was called 10/4). When the officer wasn't able to make it at the last minute due to a health complication, the other officer said to the sergeant, "I'll take King." Now I was pretty shocked. Out of everyone, he was asking me? Sure, I was strong enough to carry the bodies, but I was young. It struck me as strange that he didn't ask one of the other old-timers. Nonetheless, I was down to get the experience.

As soon as I stepped into the wagon, it was chill. All this time, I had been working the hole to leverage my time; meanwhile, this entire position was the hole! It took me off guard how calm our shift was. It was quiet as soon as you stepped into the vehicle, and there was no concern about getting the next call. The only things we had to listen for were body pick-ups or arrestee transports. All it took was one shift for me to know I needed to work this as long as possible. Unfortunately, that was made a reality due to our fellow officer having a major health condition that forced him to go on medical leave. Although titled the third man on the wagon, his sickness raised the opportunity for me to work the position. Reflecting, I knew that the wagon was a blessing in disguise. It was the hole times two. The additional free time I had was used to maximize the habits I already built as a patrol officer. I know that most guys would try to use this time to chill, but I wasn't about to give up my routine for the sake of comfort. I knew what would happen if I didn't have my new itinerary prepared like the other cops. I'd fall into the cycle of eating out more, chilling aimlessly, listening to music to no end, and only getting out the car to grab a new body.

Instead, I used my time to go in on perfecting my business plan and studying. It doesn't matter what the established order is for a specific environment. When you come in, you get to adapt it to your own needs by being bold enough to do what works for you. That doesn't mean avoiding your job duties. It means that if everyone else goes for drinks afterward, you don't have to go to build camaraderie. You can go to class, the gym, the park to study, or even a restaurant with wifi to work. Before the wagon, I had maybe four hours a day for studying and building assess-ments. After the wagon, I had nearly eight hours to grind! I knew what an opportunity looked like for me, and I made the most of it.

Of course, some people didn't agree with my decision. When the young guys saw me work-ing in the new position, they tried to clown me. They'd say things like, "Man, you're too young to be working the wagon! You aren't ever gonna get promoted! You know you can't get a higher rank working the wagon. You should be out here with us! What you're doing is for the big guys and old-timers." They saw how in shape I was and tried to associate my body with my job position. They knew I was young and thought I needed to do the same things as them. To aspire to climb the same ladder as them; to go after the same bad guys as them. Reality check, those are the same guys that ask me how to take control of their lives now. Everyone wasn't like that, though. Men like Vince knew that by taking on the paddy wagon, I was about to go to the next level. They saw how I managed my time with the hole and couldn't wait to see how I'd flip this opportunity too.

Becoming Uncomfortable For Long-Term Gains

The funny thing about all of it, when it came to do-ing the real work associated with the meat wag-on, none of us patrol officers were prepared. I re-member my first day collecting a body. This older woman called to report it, and apparently, the body had been there for days in the heat. When my partner and I arrived at the home, we got our equipment together (which only happened to be the body bag and a pair of thin gloves) and headed inside. Before we even walked in entirely, I was greeted by the foulest smell I'd ever sniffed in my life. It slapped me straight across my nose and pulled tears out of my eyes. I was unaware of how disgusting the human body could get after death, combined with humidity, heat, and several days of wasting. The old-timer began to laugh at me for being so sickened by the smell. Even as we got closer to the body, I felt less and less ready to carry it on up to the truck. Mainly because of the size of this guy. We could tell that he was a big dude before death, but he was huge, coupled with the swelling. We started to line up to the body, and I was forced to grab the head as the newcomer. Now the head is the last thing you want to grab while collecting a body because you worry about two things, the morbid look stuck on their faces plus the potential organs that might fall out of their backs. I wasn't ready for the latter because as soon as we lifted him, his entire organ system fell out of his back. I immediately ran off to discard myself of the lunch I had eaten earlier. Between not thinking I could breathe due to the stench to seeing a man's organs fall out of his back, I had had enough for one day. The old-timer just laughed at me with the excitement of a teen. I'm sure he got a good kick out of how squeamish I was in the beginning. But, this was the position. So I had to go back and make sure we got the body (the entire body) into the car. No matter if the organs had just fallen out onto the ground or what the maggots were doing inside of them.

I know you're probably reading this and wondering why I was so comfortable switching to this position. My job was to face death, carry it, and transport it to its next destination. I learned quickly that death came in all ages, shapes, sizes, and colors. Her scorn knew no boundary. In some way, it was easier facing this side of death than dealing with the dangers of being shot at. My goal wasn't to be a commemorated cop. It was to become a millionaire and to take care of my family. That meant looking at children, adults, and elders in the face as I put them in the back of the police van every day. It meant taking six or seven times to adjust to the horrific sights, using cigar ashes to put into our noses to block the smells, accepting the smell of grief would plague your uniform, and keeping hand sanitizer within reach. To pick up bodies of people who had just gotten a haircut, or who just finished their makeup. They left their homes, and we took them to the morgue. A trip to death that wasn't expected, and it was my job to ensure every piece of them made it to the medical examiner's office. Again, there wasn't anything ideal about this position change other than the time it gave me. But it was one of the greatest decisions I made back then. In the beginning, I was just the muscular guy that couldn't hold down his food. Eventually, I was able to pick up a body, clean my hands, and go right back to eating a chicken sandwich from Wendy's. If you're committed to your goals, there's absolutely nothing you can't adjust to. And if you asked me if I'd do anything differently to try and make myself more comfortable back then, I'd proudly say no. Discomfort is what allows you to recognize how not only to be grateful for the comfort you get in the long-run but how to avoid abusing it.

And, most importantly, how to not become addicted to it. Comfort flows with the seasons. The more income you have sets your bar higher, but it doesn't stop it from dropping off now and then. By choosing to be uncomfortable early on, I was prepared for the cyclic movement of comfort.

When I look at my typical day, it always included the following:

Pre-shift roll call (that we didn't have to focus on due to us working the wagon)
Sitting outside of clubs for crowd control and visibility
Visiting properties
Studying and reading
Picking up bodies
Dropping off bodies
Transporting prisoners
Working out

Because of the nature of our work, our supervisor wasn't worried about my extracurricular activities. I will say this is why you want to show up on your job well. Had I been known as a lazy employee, a bad worker, or anything else like it,

I wouldn't have had the same grace over me to build a multi-million dollar company while also working my shift. I also made sure that in some ways, my extracurriculars tied to my job. When I'd check out abandoned buildings, I would make sure that I reported them to the department. When I worked out, I justified it by having to pick up heavy bodies frequently. This is the art of finesse that doesn't steal from anyone. It allows different worlds and jobs to be able to co-exist. And these two worlds co-existed for five years. Over time I became known as Jemal The Wagon Guy. The original man never returned to his position, and I was happy to fill the role as long as possible. It gave me the freedom and liberty I needed to make even more impactful moves for my family. Note, had I been bad with my time or with making decisions, the extra time would have been of no value to me other than rest. The hole prepared me to be responsible with the undercover blessing I received.

Swift and Efficient Decisions

One thing I've always appreciated about myself is my ability to make accurate and quick decisions. It might come from being in organized sports and learning how to decide in a blink of an eye, but I know it's one of my greatest attributes. The great thing about it is that it can be trained. I became incredible with the ability to choose because of the preparation and practice. From all of the reading, studying, personal development, and athletic training, I've created a memory bank of information to pull from. That's why I don't care about your high school GPA nor your collegiate graduation status. When you have access to information, it's your job to create an in-brain library for yourself. So what, you can't afford the conference yet? Read books recommended by your favorite online teachers. Bookmark Instagram posts and create a knowledge folder. Roam through YouTube to learn various opinions, practices, and teachings. You have to learn the power of decision making so you can empower yourself to want to understand better. Over the years, I've learned that all results are the outcomes of the decisions we make based on our exposure.

Create a better environment for yourself by starting with your mind! Then ask yourself, what can you be doing more?

Typically I'll raise this question, and people respond with how busy they already are. In particular, college students. But you should be the thing that you're currently doing. There's no reason just to be a student anymore. You can be a student, a community builder, an athlete, a business owner, and anything else you desire. I know it's hard for certain people to process this because of the age-old lie, "We only work for eight hours a day." But if we have light for twelve hours, and we only need to sleep for eight, that's sixteen hours a day that we could be capitalizing on. Instead, we let them tell us that we can only make money within an eight-hour window, we can only learn in an eight-hour window; that the center of our entire life depends on this eight-hour cycle. The training starts at daycare and reaches into retirement. Reflecting over your life, what areas are you only doing what's required of you so you can just get by? How much time are you wasting? Why are you using all of your time only for a small change in compensation? No disrespect, family, but you can no longer want God to be aggressive with your blessings when you're passive with your actions. Slow feet don't get to eat champion meals! Stop letting the dreams you have when you're asleep outweigh the life you live while you're awake! Pledge to yourself that you're going to take the reigns of your life back from the world.

Think about it.

When we start elementary school, they make us learn the Pledge of Allegiance. When we go to college, they make us learn the school's fight song. When we join a company, we have to learn the mission statement. But then you treat the most prized institution—your life—like it's less than the company you work for. There's too much emphasis on a job that's sole purpose is stability, not elevation. The same applies to education. The morning instruction is creating balance while the extracurricular activities are creating your elevation. The relationship between the two matters because during the elevation you feel better, you're accomplishing more than the minimum, and you have something great going on in life. Mere stability doesn't do that. It just keeps you stable. It takes away the pressure of knowing you have a roof over your head, food to eat, and clothes to wear. None of that makes you feel like you're ready to take on the world. If anything, it can fight to keep you complacent. What are you most connected to, your destination, or your vehicle? Because the vehicle may offer you a fantastic ride, but it's never greater than the destination itself.

Chapter 12

DECISIONS BIGGER THAN YOURSELF

Before you can make decisions that benefit those around you, you'll have to be aware of the cost of yourself first. We've briefly discussed this before, but here's the formula for the cost of you.

You = Your Responsibilities (bills/liabilities) + Your Dreams + The Tools You Need

Knowing how much it takes to keep a roof over your head, food on your plate and the cost of your dreams, and the tools you'll need to achieve them creates a specific financial goal. I meet so many people who don't even know what their bare minimum cost is, i.e., how much does it cost to maintain your current standard of living. Without calculating the cost of their dream, they stumble when I ask them how much they're spending month to month on bills and discretionary spending like gas and groceries. If that's you, I need you to take a moment to download your last three months' bank statements, highlight every bill in one color, your grocery store visits and gas in another, and everything else that was optional in a third color. Then calculate each color section so you can see how much your bills are on average (over three months), how much you spend at the store/gas station, and how much you're spending on random items. After you get the number for each month and all three individual colors, you can take color one from each month, add them together, then divide it by three to get your average. Repeat the same process for color numbers two and three.

Example statement

Date	Description		Amount	Balance
Beginning Balance				1,111.00
6/8	Card Purchase	Shell Food Mart Card 0000	-5.55	1,105.45
6/12	Card Purchase	McDonald's Z0001 Franklin IN Card 0000	-6.95	1,098.50
6/12	Card Purchase	Shell Food Mart Card 0000	-10.21	1,088.29
6/15	Card Purchase	Nissan Fin. Card 0000	-289.74	798.55

Your level of awareness of how much your life costs determines the efficiency of your actions. If you have no idea the set number you need to keep your life functioning the same (at minimum), how will you know when you've overspent outside of getting an overdraft fee or a late notice? The cost of you sets boundaries for everything you do. Not only are you able to manage the money you have today better, but you're ready to make more sound decisions for tomorrow. To be specific, it calculates your next move for you. Take what you bring in every month, then subtract it from your personal cost, and you'll see what you have left-over to put back into your dreams. Note, this is the beginning of transforming into someone capable of making decisions outside of themselves.

While you're learning your numbers and adjusting to respecting your new budget, I encourage you to focus on envisioning your future. Envision what you need to do. How will you feel after finally reaching your goal? When you go to Google to look up the definition of envision it says, "to imagine as a future possibility; visualize." The very act of envisioning something is to see what something would be like in a different season than now. I've found this to be the key to my days.

If you'd ask me if I visualize my future, I'd respond by saying all day, every day, and especially before I go to sleep. I call my practice the Wish Received, and I've been doing it for years. What I like to do is:

Lay down and clear my mind of negative thoughts
Protect my space by making sure no one's bringing me negativity
Close my eyes
I breathe at a calm and steady pace
I begin to see myself receiving the thing I'm currently wishing aka working for
I bask in the feelings that come with manifesting that thing

No matter how hardworking you are, how focused you believe yourself to be, or how determined you present to be, we're all chasing after certain sets of feelings. It's the feeling of the thing you've wanted that drives you to get it. If something doesn't feel right, it won't push you to go hard for it. Even when we think of losing weight, we go hard not because of the feeling of beating your body up and being sore for days. We go hard because of the feelings of satisfaction and accomplishment attached to training and losing the weight. Of course, we aren't to be led by our emotions, but they're huge indicators of whether or not we're doing something that honors our desires, dreams, and vision.

Self-actualizing my dreams before bed puts me in so many different scenarios, outcomes, and examples; that they almost don't have any option but to manifest themselves. The same way an athlete tries to think of every scenario possible prior to coming against an opponent, I think of every possible outcome for my life. Before I make any move, I'm asking myself:

What are all the obstacles that might pop-up?
What are the resources I need?
Do I have those resources?
Do I know anyone that does?
What's my objective for this move?
Who will this impact?
What are the risks?
What are some potential unknown risks?
What will this accomplishment feel like?

Most people only deal with reality. They build their lives on pillars that they can see and touch.

They use quotes like, "Reality is real." The saying is cute, but it's not entirely true. I prefer to deal with what's to come. Our lives have proven that reality is nothing more than the result of your imagination. Let's think about it. The phone you have next to you was once a thought in someone's mind. They wondered what the world would be like if we were able to be anywhere in the world, and still be able to speak to someone that we knew. So they dreamt up a scenario in which this could be a reality, and they applied pressure until it was one. The chair you're sitting on is the fruit of someone's innovation. They saw a design in their minds and worked to manifest it in real life. There is absolutely nothing we see that's made by a man's hands that wasn't a mere thought at first. Even God had to take what was in His consciousness and declare it to exist in our realm. And if we're made in His likeness, that means our thoughts are powerful too.

So although the quotes are cute and Instagrammable, the truth is that your imagination is what's real, not reality. It is all made up of the evidence of ideas coming to fruition; of the hard work it takes to press towards a vision that doesn't have any real fruit yet. Not letting go when the odds are betting against the dreams you dream and can't fully explain. See, being committed to reality is way too easy, and that's what the average person does. They're committed to what they can see in real life.

They judge their marriage on their parents.

They make as much money as they've seen.
They love who they believe they should love.
They eat meals they've seen eaten before.
They travel to places they've been to.

It's in your ability to be committed to something that doesn't physically exist that allows you to dictate what you settle for and engage with daily. This is why children are so amazing. They see colors that don't exist. They sing songs with words that haven't been written. They play spy games in the backyard like they're in a country that sits in outer space. They see things that adults can't see because they haven't been conditioned to become realists. If I gave any advice that you adhered to for this chapter, it's not to let go of your inner kid. Being grown is overrated and draining. I'm not saying to speak or spend money like a child, I'm reminding you to tap into that zeal for living that you used to have. To expect the unexpected and to wish for the unrealistic. To lay down for thirty minutes before bed and envision what it would feel like and mean to get precisely what you wanted. To allow that what to be so big that you know it's a stretch even to receive it.

Your imagination is the preview for things to come. It goes back to the movie theatre example I used before. Seeing the last fifteen minutes before watching the rest of the movie gives you an unfair advantage. You manage your emotions better, you're in less of a shock at specific outcomes, and you no longer have to prepare for the result. Imagination allows you to create those last fifteen minutes for your own life and to act accordingly. That's why it's so sweet when you get it! The end of a thing is greater than its beginning (Ecclesiastes 7:8) and you always set the outcome from the beginning! Your words dictate what's to come. What comes is always greater (positively or negatively) than what was originally there. Think about your life, like throwing an event. The idea for the event is never greater than the game itself. Your dream isn't to have a thought; it's to have a thought that gets actualized. Yet, fear of the unknown, the unseen, and the unpredictable keep you from operating in the realm of imagination. Fear is killing your inner-child, thus making your day-to-day mundane and cold. So you try to escape by not dealing with your mind.

Escaping The Future By Ignoring The Present

Because thoughts are powerful, no matter if they're positive or negative, we become what we do when we try to escape. Now I get it. Most don't classify their life routines as escapism. They might not recognize that regularly consuming TV, social media, taking a nap, eating all day, avoiding hard conversations and not thinking about what's to come, can be seen as a means to ignore the present. They look at these actions as standard parts of their days, thus not paying it any mind. If you have a smartphone, you can see how much you escape on average by looking at your daily screen time. How many hours are you giving to Instagram when you say you don't have time to work on a business model? How often are you on YouTube, and how much of it is professional, spiritual, or emotional development?

Someone asked me why I think it's easy for people to escape life instead of building on it. I genuinely believe it's because it's inherently easier. We get different opportunities to flex our perseverance muscles growing up. From deciding whether or not we're sticking with an activity after it becomes more challenging, to the way we cope after loss... Depending on the choices we make in various circumstances, our quitting muscle is either strengthened or weakened. Based on conversations with people, I believe most are being conditioned to strengthen their quitting muscles because people live their lives based on preferences and emotions. If they don't feel like it any longer, then they're over it. There isn't an internal process that happens that helps decipher if this is the best decision to make in the long-term.

Plus, they aren't raised with examples of what building looks like outside of a 9 to 5. You couple being a master quitter with a lack of exposure, and escaping is the easiest route. In reality, people don't want to deal with the responsibility associated with their desired change. So they give up on their health, eventually themselves; they let go of their dreams and settle for a career. Everything about them becomes about self no matter if they're married or with kids. That's why mastering the art of decision making before having a family is critical. So if you decide to build one, you're making decisions that are bigger than yourself.

Family Leveled Me Up

I made the decision that I wanted a family while I was a kid. Even when I made my millionaire declaration at eight, I saw a family connected to that. I'm sure it's because of my amazing parents and the community I grew up in because I never saw myself just living on my own. I wanted the wife, the kids, the whole nine. When Camille and I first started dating in high school, we were already discussing our childrens' names, parental duties, philosophies and our future life. By the time we got married, we knew that every decision we were making would impact us, but they were ultimately for the betterment of our childrens' children. Considering that, we bought a house that could fit a family in it before she was pregnant. We set up accounts for them; we created a daycare center that would educate them. We studied, read, asked our parents questions, anything to get us ready for the entrance of new life.

You can imagine my excitement when Camille told me she was pregnant the first time. Man. It was late December in 2003, and she cooked an exquisite dinner. I was excited over the food alone. We had a pleasant conversation, and in the middle of us sitting there, she pulls out a pregnancy stick and tells me it's positive. I was ecstatic! I remember saying, "I got a lot of work to do!" Not only was I married to the woman of my dreams, but I was about to become a father! Our 4,000 square foot greystone became all the more special that night. With tears in my eyes, I began to reflect on how we'd been talking about legacy all these years, and now it's finally here. Whatever gender the baby was didn't even matter. It was our first kid of three, and we were happy to welcome them home. That revelation shifted my mind from grinding for a family that's on its way; to grinding for a family that's here.

The months to come were smooth sailing for Camille. She didn't experience any complications, morning sickness, or anything else like it. She looked amazing as her body transformed into the first home of our child. I was proud that I was able to retire her before the pregnancy, so she could do what she wanted to do. She could wake up when she needed to, get the nutrients her body craved and so forth. Once we found out we were having our first daughter; we got to work. We brought in professional artists to create a mural in her room, decked out the place with princess decorations, filled up her closet with clothes of all sizes for different growth phases. We put scriptures on the wall so she'd learn she's not just our princess, but she was God's princess too. Many gifts poured in for her because she was Camille's parents' first grandchild and my parents' fifth. She had everything she could ever need before she got to her second home.

Then she came.

It was in the middle of the night, and I was working my shift when Camille called and said her water broke. Now, I wasn't too keen on how long labor could last, so I just knew we only had a few minutes before she'd be giving birth. I told my partner Vince and the lieutenant that my baby girl was on the way. He instructed me to take the squad car to get home, so we did. As soon as we got there, my neighbor and fellow officer/ best friend named Tony met us at my house. He had on his full uniform just like me, and we ran inside to get Camille and the baby bag. Once we loaded up the car, Tony turned on his police lights and sirens, and we rushed to the hospital. It was the middle of the night, so there wasn't any traffic. Yet, he still drove as if the hospital wasn't less than 2 miles from our house. We pulled right up to the ER, and we hurried inside. The staff wondered if there was an emergency because all they could see were two male officers freaking out over this woman being in labor. We made all that noise to ensure Camille was treated properly and swiftly, all for her to be in labor for over twenty-four hours. It wasn't funny then, but I'm able to laugh about it now. I thought it was going to be a few minutes and bam; we'd have our daughter. The heavens always have a different say than us, though.

What started as a natural pregnancy quickly turned into a stormy labor that led to Camille having to get a C-section. She fought it at first, but she had been in labor for too long. For her and the baby, it would be safer to move forward with the procedure. We had a few seconds to mourn the idea of a traditional birth before she was dressed and ready to go. After a short while, our daughter was finally here, but things hadn't gone as we'd hoped for.

Our daughter, Ayanna, didn't come out crying. Naturally, the doctors went into action to see if she was having any complications with breathing. Because of that, she's my only child who's umbilical cord I wasn't able to cut, a ritual that represents the complete transition from her mommy's womb to being entirely dependent on our decisions in this natural world. But in the middle of the doctor's helping our child, Camille held my hand and told me that she felt like she was nearing death. I can't describe that feeling. Being such a strong man but, in an instant, become so vulnerable and without any ability to help. I prayed that God could see the two most important people in my life and keep them here. The emotions were crashing down on me like a tidal wave until finally, baby girl cried. Somehow her cry was the confirmation I needed to know that they'd both be okay. August 26, 2004, became a day of testimony, and it proved the existence of miracles for me.

Four short years later, we'd be back to do it all over again for Jasmine. Now, Ayanna was born right before we hit millionaire status, but Jasmine was born afterward. That in itself allowed us to prepare slightly differently, especially since we knew Camille was going to choose a C-section. When Camille was pregnant with Jazzy, we started to feel the pressure of wondering what sex our baby would be. It was different than our first child because we knew we wanted three kids and a mix of girls and boys. How the combination happened didn't bother us then. But now, things were different. It wasn't that we'd be angry with either or, but it would have been so smooth to have had a boy the second go-round and leave the third option open. Jasmine wasn't having that, though. When we were at the doctor's office and learned we were having our second daughter, we were both happy; I'd be lying if I said I didn't feel pressured to make sure our third child was a son.

Camille and I are planners. That's even with the things that people say we shouldn't try to plan. Learning about the second pregnancy gave me fuel for the third and gratefulness that we were able to do this two times already. Our thoughts about a son were fleeting because we were preparing for becoming parents times two. We chose her name based on a name I picked in high school. I knew if I had a daughter, I wanted her to be named Jasmine, and if I had a son, I wanted a junior. With no surprise as I look back, Jasmine came into this world as unique as we could imagine on March 10, 2008. Now, this labor didn't include any extravagant police entrance. With planned C-sections, you set an appointment for your delivery date. We arrived in peace and were ready to get the show on the road. Again, Jasmine wasn't having any of that either. From the moment she was born, she came out with the lungs of a lioness. She had zero complications, and I was able to cut her umbilical cord. Camille was fine this time. Everything felt like it was going to be a breeze until Jasmine wouldn't stop crying. For context, Ayanna was a quiet baby.

After her first cry, she was ready to eat and sleep for the rest of the night. You can imagine our surprise when we had a rather calm birth, and Jasmine came prepared to rip the walls down. I knew then that she had my temperament. Let me tell you; that girl cried until 4 a.m. I was so tired that I was watching Camille as I held Jas thinking how we just finished a fight. Eventually, the nurse came and realized we still hadn't gone to sleep. She asked if we wanted to take her to the nursery, and with Ayanna, we would've said no. But we were so tired we responded with a resounding yes and got some well-needed sleep. I had officially become a father to two princesses of different personalities.

Ironically enough, Jas ended up being the one that came with me to visit properties, play in the dirt and help put together furniture. She and her sister became two of the strongest motivations I ever had outside of their mother. I tell everyone this, becoming a family man helped me with business. Talking about starting a family and having a family kicks you into a different drive. You see their needs and how feeble they are and realize you're 120% responsible for their lives. What they do and don't need to see a therapist for lies in how you raise them, teach them, speak to them, and love them. Taking on the role of parent of two put Camille and I into a new gear. Mainly because being a spouse and a parent requires a level of focus you don't get in your single years. I'm not saying that you should get married and have kids solely to elevate in business. I'm saying that these two things help you leverage your business! Too many people look at marriage and children as weights when in reality, they're fuel.

It's crazy because Camille and I never struggled with wondering if we'd be fit parents. We were both raised with amazing parents with solid faith foundations. That, plus the years we spent working on getting ready for their entrance into our lives, helped us be confident in knowing we were built for this. All we cared about was family and service. Everything else was vain. Again, we spent years preparing for them. Just them! We didn't have to make any abrupt decisions because of being ill-prepared. This is why I push financial security as hard as I do. Money may not buy happiness, but it sure does create environments that do. Even when it comes to transitioning from being a husband to a husband and a father, the money helped ease the blow.

I'm sure you know that being a spouse means 100% of your energy goes to the other person. What they need, desire, aspire for, and vice versa. Becoming a spouse and a parent puts you in a predicament where you have to learn how to give 100% to each person. Learning that because we're unique and so are our roles, our

100% should look different for everyone, and it's always changing. Camille took the reins with this, and she transformed so elegantly into a mother. For me, she balanced everything perfectly. Camille remained my wife while fully stepping into becoming a mother. Having the daycare helped a lot because she was able to run the business and take care of the babies. We had created a win-win situation for ourselves through one of our business endeavors. We knew and accepted that the babies were the focus, and we were a team. The changes that occurred turned us into even better people.

After we had the two of them, I became softer and more understanding. Raising daughters helped me with being able to empathize with others on a deeper level. It also helped me become aware of the words I speak over people's lives. These two shifts helped me make better decisions. Coupled with knowing I couldn't make decisions as risky as we could before the kids, my ability to calculate long-term impact increased. Before, Camille and I might be willing to take a risk on an opportunity that no one would even think about. But now I was thinking things like, "I've got these two little ones, and they need a father." It allowed me to become more aware of the calls I took on the job and the opportunities I'd invest in. I believe the reason I didn't regret having to do this is that Camille and I were financially prepared for this shift in lifestyle. We didn't wait on kids to figure out the risks we wanted to take. We took them before. Legacy had only become more tangible, and the shifts that came with it were blessings, not pitfalls.

There isn't anything special about us that allows us to think outside of ourselves and our current reality. Making sound decisions is a learned behavior not a genetic trait. It must be practiced. It's like working out and training your muscle fibers to become more efficient when firing off. In the beginning, your muscles use every neuron possible to contract and relax. That's why you're so sore in those first few weeks. Over time, your muscles learn how to equip themselves for performing specific movements—making your muscles stronger. Our minds are the same. We might fall for a lot of things in the beginning. We might settle for subpar decisions. But as we continue to feed ourselves sound information and test our ability to reason, we become more effective decision-makers. So, in reality, you're not a bad decision maker just because; you have not because you train not. By the time we need to make decisions that extend far beyond our own lives, we've become masters.

Even when my children ask me questions, I always ask them what they think about it first. My goal is to empower them to trust their deductive reasoning before looking to other people for answers. That way, they can spot faulty thinking on their own when Camille and I pass on. It's the same thing I want for you. My goal is to help you become so amazing at making decisions that your life gets easier, and your mind gets clearer.

That's how you'll be able to tap into our final pillar of this book. Legacy is built on the back of strong decision making. It's not just about making babies and taking care of them. And it's not just about starting a business in your thirties and making it your life's work. It's about being able to go outside of yourself, even your blood, and make decisions that'll influence the lives of those you won't know in thirty years. That occurs after you're able to make decisions that have positive long-term consequences.

MILLIONAIRE MOMENTS

Today I want you to reflect on these questions:

Have you been making decisions that are outside of yourself? In what ways have you been selfish in your decision making? How can you shift your mind to start paying attention to the decisions you make on a daily basis?

After taking a moment to reflect, feel free to write down your answer somewhere safe. You can even share it with me by sending me a message on Instagram: @9to5millionaire.

Chapter 13

REDEFINING LEGACY

In the morning sow thy seed, and in the evening withhold not thine hand: for thou knowest not whether shall prosper, either this or that, or whether they both shall be alike good.
Ecclesiastes 11:6

The first time I read that verse, I remember thinking about how much time we let pass us because of cultural norms. This piece of scripture is literally telling us how important multiple streams of income are. The writer encourages us to work in the morning and not become idle in the evening, so we have options for harvest time. No matter how many amazing things we've done as humans, we're still mere creations. That means that we can only think so far ahead and from a limited number of perspectives. We cannot force seeds to grow or harvest to yield ripened fruit. We cannot dictate the wind or demand that the waves of the sea come crashing down. The only thing we can control is increasing the probability of winning by trying continually. Yet, we treat our lives as if we know exactly what the future holds and what we'll reap in the unfolding process.

We go home and waste our lives away by watching YouTube and Netflix. We eat and sleep, just to get back up and do it all over again. Limiting ourselves to thinking we can only work and study within an eight-hour window has crippled us. Solely viewing ourselves as workers rather than royalty has enabled our limited thinking to continue. When have you ever heard of a king clocking out by five? Do they take off their title and become a peasant for the remainder of their day? No, they're royalty 24/7, which means they'll have responsibilities to tend to all day. As someone reading this, you should be operating the same. Time is of the essence for everyone, but mainly you. You can't put in all the work and self-analyze just to continue to make decisions that don't uplift you or your loved ones.

Do you believe you have a legacy of greatness tethered to you? Act like it. Work your work in the morning and keep your hands moving in the evening. Prove Ecclesiastes 11:6 to be true for yourself by giving your legacy a higher chance at winning. That's what took my life to the next level. When I was introduced to real estate, I realized that I was playing a game of rinse and repeat. The more I could repeat the process of buying a unit to fix then sell for profit, the more I could perfect the formula. By the time I was thirty years old, I had at least thirty units to my name. I can't recall the number of properties, but I know I had a building for every bill I had. When it was time to consider investing in a new building, I'd also ask myself, "What's your desired monthly cash flow for the next property? Questions like that helped me create a clear action plan for real estate and create examples like this one for my audience to use. For those who have been wanting to create a simple strategy for investing in properties, I want you to get these first five units to start.

Unit #1 - Cashflow Property $1,500
▸ Pays your home mortgage or rent
Unit #2 - Cashflow Property $500
▸ Pays your car payment
Unit #3 - Cashflow Property $1,000
▸ Pays your food expenses
Unit #4 - Cashflow Property $500
▸ Pays your health expenses
Unit #5 - Cashflow Property $1,000
▸ Pays your lifestyle expenses

Once you have these, I want you to focus on the different investments you want to make and acquire a building for each idea. Sticking to this process got me to $17,000 net cash flow every month by thirty. This kind of system allowed Camille and me to say—forget the banks! We became the bank! My properties have become my bank accounts, filling up every month like clockwork, and always there when I need them. Setting yourself up financially to build a legacy is honestly about flipping the same hustle so often that you become the it person for it. That not only builds up your bank account, but it also builds up your confidence to succeed.

When we were denied the loan to start the daycare, we didn't think all hope was lost. Our initial thought wasn't to beg the bank for a loan; we immediately went to the bricks. I was twenty-nine at this point, and we were ready for a family business that Camille could help run. Finding out that we couldn't get a loan because we lacked business experience in running a daycare probably would've stopped most people. But we had been grinding for years in real estate. At this point, you couldn't tell us we weren't capable of doing something. Our faith was so strong that we turned back to real estate to create a solution for starting the childcare centers. To be exact, we self-invested $250,000 into acquiring a building and renovating it for our launch. We saved up by purchasing investment properties to flip, then using 50% of the profits to put toward another flip, and 50% toward the improvements of the daycare center. It took us a total of two-and-a-half years of investing to reach our target.

By the time we launched, we were in full swing. We knew nothing about daycares. Within two months, we had over fifty children in that business! In an industry that the bank said would fail and the original building-owner said it didn't make sense for the neighborhood. Those fifty kids were bringing in $40,000 a month, within a year, that building started generating well over seven figures a year. Next thing we knew, our net worth climbed to nearly three million dollars. Between thirty and thirty-five, the only additional stream of income was the daycare centers. My day-to-day included being a husband, a father, an officer, a real estate investor, and a co-founder with Camille. We ensured we were intentional with each stream before looking to add another

one, including my advancement at the department. You know, every time the Chicago Police
Department offered a promotional test, I bought
a property. With two daughters and a wife to
care for, I wanted my time to be spent with them.
I cared less about rank on the force or moving on
up. With higher position comes great responsibility and time capacity. I had a goal for working at
the department. I wasn't caught up on their goals
for me. That's how we have to treat our jobs. You
can't let them have so much control over your
life that the checks they give you dictate where
you live, how you live and what you drive or what
school your kids attend. You were meant to be
fastened to your mission, not an establishment.

Keeping our streams simple created the opportunity for our additional revenue to be micro-
streams of what we already had. For example,
real estate is a stream of income, but every single
unit is a micro-stream. Even the daycares had mi-
cro-streams connected to it. One daycare might
have a capacity of 100 kids, so I thought, *These
are 100 potential tenants.*" They trusted us with
their most prized possessions, why wouldn't they
trust us with where they lived? I started buying
up properties near the daycare and pitched our
rental company to the parents. Even some of our
staff began to rent with us because of the level of
rapport we built. These are the things that happen when you do everything with a spirit of excellence. As you continue to pave your path, new
steps will form to make your journey worthwhile.
It's due to the culmination of all of this work that
prepares you for legacy building.

Build It In The Present, Reap It In The Future

When I hear the word legacy, I hear next in line. As a family man, that meant my two children, plus my soon-to-come third child. For you, it could mean your kids too, or the community you wish to leave an impact on. To intentionally build a legacy, it means to set up the next person deliberately. Legacy isn't about you per se. You reap the benefits of what you made while you're establishing it. Others obtain the benefits of what you created once it's complete and set in stone. It is the process of helping to bring up people who'll be better than you and those you're preparing to take over. It represents your name and all that you accomplished while breathing, and the work that continues to flow after you've stopped. It's the walk to becoming a better version of yourself to acquire the necessary favor that'll open doors for people simply by mentioning your name. Legacy is simply the ramifications of the decisions you made that led to the stories that'll be told about you when you're not around.

When you make decisions with this in mind, you'll naturally turn your money into a relay race. You'll be passing on wealth to the next generation so they can run further and faster than you! That is the goal. What are you currently passing on to the next generation? Is it doubt? Fear of losing? Anxiety? Debt? What are the things you're handing down right now (even outside your relationship with your money)? Although few will admit to it, so many of us live for ourselves rather than thinking bigger. By the time I get to talk to someone that's blue-collar about their definition of legacy, the wording sounds similar, but its foundation is entirely different.

People like me always think greater than, but blue-collar settles for equal to. Instead of thinking about handing down ten million dollars to their grandchildren, they focus on being able to hand down a position on their job or an entry to their alma mater. Thus, leaving other people in control of their children's lives. That company isn't forced by law to hire your son, or is it required to employ your daughter. That university you attended doesn't even have to give them a discounted rate. The two things blue-collar workers see as significant advancements could be taken away in the blink of an eye. Legacy is and should remain personal. Others shouldn't be able to dictate the outcome of what you've worked hard for. Even when I think of my own family, my father couldn't understand my career decisions because they didn't come with corporate rank and hierarchy. I was a multi-millionaire sure, but what did that mean? What was I passing down to my children in terms of respecting titles and authority? It took some time for my people to see that what I was giving them was far greater than any potential job opportunity.

It's purely survival mode that encourages you to say, "I want to give them what I had." instead of "I'm going to give them a 100 times better chance than I had." If we break it down in terms of numbers, legacy is the ability to multiply something that you did before passing it on down or over. Remember what the master said to the servant that hid his one talent out of fear of losing it?

"His master replied, 'You wicked, lazy servant! So you knew that I harvest where I have not sown and gather where I have not scattered seed? Well then, you should have put my money on deposit with the bankers, so that when I returned, I would have received it back with interest."'So take the bag of gold from him and give it to the one who has ten bags. For whoever has will be given more, and they will have an abundance. Whoever does not have, even what they have will be taken from them. And throw that worthless servant outside, into the darkness, where there will be weeping and gnashing of teeth.'
Matthew 25:26-30

All that servant tried to do was return what had been given to him. Yet, it cursed him for the rest of his life and lineage because he couldn't discern the importance of investing! What is the use of having a talent if you refuse to multiply it? You have then become a wasteful vessel, unable to improve upon the lives of those around you. It's similar to being flatlined. You're moving throughout life as if you were already dead. The most fantastic thing about being human, though, is our ability to pivot. So what if you've been in survival mode since you were a child. Who cares if you hadn't built a grand legacy by forty? As long as those lungs of yours are still exchanging carbon dioxide and oxygen, you have the opportunity to get it right. Practically, you can start by working your job and saving 20-30% of your total income. Take these savings and buy positive cash flow producing properties. Then, let your investments fund your dream life. Don't try and make it harder than it is either. Get disciplined with your savings and develop a strategy on how to use them!

By the time I was a multi-millionaire, I was still using my cop salary with intention. Every two weeks, I'd take my check to the bank and divide it between my daughters' future tuition accounts. It didn't become money to use frivolously just because I could. Like every other dollar I make, it had a job to do. Honestly, being able to move like this came from my ability to understand you get out everything you put in. From a child, I was able to see that if I didn't treat something seriously, it would create its destination outside of the one I intended. When I reached my twenties, I knew I needed to believe and work for unlimited opportunities to come my way. In my thirties, I saw the blessing of this combined faith and works mentality. By thirty-five, I knew that everything was mine for the taking; I just had to take it. However, there was one major obstacle that seemed like I couldn't get over, and that was the birth of my son.

Believe Without Ceasing

Everything in my life seemed to be aligning except the actualization of my son. I had my wife, my daughters, our home, the income, and the network. But there was nothing I could do in my physical nature to bring forth Jemal King Jr. For the second time, I was vulnerable and unable to force any solution to work. In 2009, Camille and I began trying to conceive him. Having a family of three with a son included wasn't up for debate. At first, everyone was supportive of the faith we had for a son this third go-round. Of course, there were playful jokes about getting another daughter, but I knew in my soul that this last seat in the kingdom we were building was for a son. Not being able to depend on my finances or anyone else during this time forced me to have to depend on my faith in God altogether. There were no back-up options, and we couldn't call anyone to force it to happen. This was a divine test to see if I was willing to tap into the measure of faith given to me at birth. I was being shown that faith is the building block to creating a real legacy.

Now faith is the substance of things hoped for,
the evidence of things not seen.
Hebrews 11:1

After several months of trying, loved ones began to say things like:

Well, maybe God just wants y'all to have your daughters.

You know you can't force God to give you a son.

If you all stopped trying for a son, maybe you two would get pregnant again. Take what you're given.

Y'all are already blessed with two kids; some people can't even have one.

It's okay if y'all are just a family of four. There's nothing wrong with that.

It would stir up my spirit to hear them doubting what I knew was a God-ordained thing. So after the first year passed, then the second, the third, and so on, you can imagine how crazy they were looking at us. My parents understood what it felt like to have to conceive a child through faith because they went through it with me. But other well-intentioned voices were trying to bring us enough sense to stop. Little did they know how hard I would go. Once we got over the hump of the first three years with no results, I let myself go even harder. We began to prepare his room, I bought a urinal for his restroom that I built just for him, and then I started to write letters to him to document the journey to his birth. I even put boy clothes in his closet!

I realized this battle wasn't going to be for the swift. This was the kind of fighting made for those that can endure. When everything seems like it's saying no... when every door is closing, and you have nothing else to do but give up or to walk in faith, you see who you are. People began to question my sanity because I decided I wasn't going to give up. For a brief moment, even Camille started to wonder whether we were doing the right thing. God brought me to the point where I couldn't listen to doctors, friends, family, or anybody else because He said it would be done. And if God said it, then it didn't matter what everyone else said. So I continued to write my letters to him. I kept his room clean and updated. I spoke to his sisters as if he would be here soon. God was showing me that anything I didn't have wasn't a question of His power, but it showed how much more faith I still needed to hold on to. Matthew 9:29 says, "According to your faith, be it unto you!" How was I supposed to declare verses like, "All things are possible to those that believe..." if I wasn't exercising it daily? Like many others, I'd be a hypocrite, touting verses with no intention of testing them to be true.

I know God brings every human to something similar. It's not because He's on a power trip either. Rewire your brain from that lie. We hit obstacles that won't move unless we have mustard seed faith because it allows us to tap into the strength the Bible says we have access to. Mark 9:23 tells us that all things could realize themselves in our lives if we simply knew that they could. There is a power that's inside of us that's connected to God Himself. I believe it was transferred when He gave His breath to Adam, and he came to life. This is why the Word says to count it all joy when trials and tribulations come! During these difficult times, we can lean into the authority of God to magnify and use our weaknesses.

With our individualistic culture, we've forgotten the power of unity and even tribes. If men can come together to create something the world has never seen before, how much more when we partner with the Most High? So often, we try to depend on our own money and status not realizing these things are crushing our faith. The journey to having my son showed me that if I could stay determined in believing he would be alive one day, then every other area of my life would be blessed. As I labored in my faith, God was revealing Himself to me. With each revelation, I was taking scripture and making it practical! Instead of reading Abraham's name while studying his faith, I'd recite my name.

18 When everything was hopeless, Abraham (Jemal) believed anyway, deciding to live not on the basis of what he saw he couldn't do but on what God said he would do. And so he was made father of a multitude of peoples. God himself said to him, "You're going to have a big family, (Jemal) Abraham!" 19 Abraham didn't focus on his own impotence and say, "It's hopeless. This hundred-year-old body could never father a child." Nor did he survey Sarah's decades of infertility and give up. 20 He didn't tiptoe around God's promise asking cautiously skeptical questions. He plunged into the promise and came up strong, ready for God, 21 sure that God would make good on what He had said.
Romans 4:18-21

By faith (Jemal) obeyed when he was called to go out to the place which he would receive as an inheritance. And he went out, not knowing where he was going. By faith he dwelt in the land of promise as in a foreign country, dwelling in tents with Isaac and Jacob, the heirs with him of the same promise; for he waited for the city which has foundations, whose builder and maker is God.
Hebrews 11:8-10

I'd go through every scripture that talked about faith and included my name. I realized that God was waiting for me to see my life the way He planned it out. That would require me to take His word literally and to put it to the test. He didn't need me just to want my son. I had to believe in my son! The difference between believing and wanting is action. When you believe, you work in great expectation and anticipation of that thing. It's like knowing a concert is coming to town, so you buy your tickets, prepare your outfit, and drive there on the day. But when you just want something, you're not required to do anything to make it happen. There's no preparation required. You're allowed to waver to the left and the right because there's no foundation for you to stand on. That's why I got the urinal, something he wouldn't be able to use until years after his birth. The room, the mural painted inside and even the clothes. There wasn't any other option. I trusted in the Word of God. Not man, not my doubts, not a doctor's advice, just God. A desire for my son might've started the journey off, but

I had to transition into faith to continue on the road quickly laid ahead for us. When you seriously believe in something, you prepare a place for it *before* its arrival!

Because what is the point in preparing for a legacy that you don't believe is coming to pass? It takes faith to write out a will before having any children. It takes faith to buy a house with extra rooms in it. It takes faith to start a business with no customers. It takes faith to go for a career you have no experience in. It takes faith to call yourself a husband, and you're not even dating yet. Everything that extends outside of ourselves requires faith, especially setting up your legacy. Knowing that my son was coming applied pressure behind the deals I was landing, the work I was doing, and even how I was raising my daughters. It made me a better husband by putting me in a position to encourage my wife when outside voices made her question God's promise. Believing in something higher than material possession will strengthen every area of your life. There's no way you can even try to compartmentalize faith. That's like trying to make your core stronger and thinking it isn't going to assist your body. Praying, hoping, and working for my son's arrival for seven years made me a man that I didn't even anticipate becoming. The person I am now and the legacy I've been able to build are due to God-honoring obedience and being faithful. So when Junior got here, I knew the next stretch of my life would be taken to a whole other level because I would no longer walk by sight, only by faith!

Chapter 14

FULL CIRCLE MOMENTS

If you were to compare me to a superhuman, I'd want people to list my greatest superpower as faith. Not my ability to amass wealth, not my physical and mental strength, but the secret weapon I've been harnessing since I was first brought into this world. I believe that my parents' having to pray me into existence embedded faith into my very DNA, thus creating my superhuman origin story. I understood at a young age that life already comes with enough obstacles. So when you couple in hard-times with self-doubt you're breeding a lifetime full of defeat, anguish, and self-pity. Honestly, if you cannot even believe in your ability to overcome the known hardships your family faces due to generational trauma, what do you think you're going to do when the unthinkable happens? You can't believe in becoming happy, yet you think you're prepared for the day a loved one gets a terminal illness? Faith doesn't even work like that. It's a muscle that has to be used consistently, and unlike our actual muscle fibers, it doesn't require any rest periods! You can relentlessly believe in a thing, and you'll only make yourself more equipped to receive it later.

I remember being a child and reading my Bible like it was speaking to me specifically. Not that I understood weighty doctrines like the Melchizedek Order or Immaculate Conception, but I was genuinely interested in consuming the biographies of the forefathers and foremothers of the faith. To know that we were still reading about these people, not fictional characters, several thousands of years later, was one of the first examples of how faith impacts legacy for me. No one ever saw Jacob wrestle that angel, but we know it happened via the scriptures. None of us witnessed Joseph try and serve Mary a bill of divorce, yet we got the inside scoop into how broken his heart was. Not a single one of us nor our recent ancestors met John The Baptist, but we recognize him as the greatest prophet born of a man and a woman. All because each of them had faith (or Emunah as they would've called it), we read their stories and cleave to their lessons. I'm not sure when it clicked for me, but eventually, I got to the point where I realized we could be doing the same thing for generations to come. When you reflect on the scriptures, they're God-inspired journals. David wrote Psalms from a place of confession. We saw how greatly loved and covered he knew he was by his Heavenly Father in Psalms 91 while also seeing how much he hated the wicked in Psalms 109. All he did was lay himself bare and submitted to the order of repentance and faith; now, we teach about him almost every other assembly service.

What do you think would happen if we did the same? If we lived our lives in such a way that people 100 years from now would be able to glean understanding from the decisions we made today? This isn't a far-fetched concept, either. We still talk about Marcus Garvey, Harriet Tubman, Ida B. Wells, Booker T. Washington, etc. as though they were alive and visiting our homes today. We know about the work they did to sacrifice for racial equity, how they commanded and inspired entire movements, and we feel the ramifications of their commitments. But because people lack the faith to believe they can create a change with themselves, they rob future generations of the opportunity to learn, cleave, and level-up. Imagine if Ida B. Wells never picked up a pen because she lost both of her parents before turning seventeen? Imagine if she thought she wasn't worthy enough to write about the lynchings she witnessed because she was a Black woman born into slavery? Without Ida, we'd have very little information on the atrocious acts of lynching and documentation to prove who prime targets were. A woman with no parents to see her through adulthood in a time where her existence was seen as a crime, had enough faith to trust in using her voice. Now we recognize her as a leading 19th-century activist, even honoring her in 2020 with a Pulitzer Prize for being courageous enough to document the violence committed against African-Americans in the era of lynching.

Every time we bet on ourselves to do our passions, we create an opportunity for change far beyond what we could have foreseen. That's why faith is the substance of things hoped for and evidence of things unseen. It creates these pockets of glimpsing into the future, and the more you tap into it, the clearer the picture becomes. You're sharpening your faith and your vision every moment you take action toward a goal that has yet to manifest. It's the combination of this kind of faith coupled with favor that allows me to see the closeness of my story and that of Joseph the son of Jacob. He was given a vision and he had the faith to receive it. At the end of his story, he's able to take care of not only his family but the families of every nation that was depending on the resources he stored up in Egypt. Essentially, Joseph's blessings weren't even about him. They were about sustaining everyone that he could. That's the kind of impact that comes with believing the picture you saw before the world tried to crush your vision.

I know if something exists or not merely by whether or not I have the faith for it. I take the "... on earth as it is in heaven..." scripture literally! All the evidence you need to continue focusing on a target is the faith to believe it's possible. That's it! If you can see it with your eyes, it's possible. Especially as humans, we aren't even the creators of the galaxy; so if we can envision something, then it must be capable of existing on this earth. Getting yourself to the point where you can say, "I believe, therefore, I receive,"— will open doors and knock down barriers you've been battling your entire life. And it's not because of some magical essence of faith. It's because real faith requires real work. Anytime you say you want something you're placing the goal outside of yourself. It now becomes an external experience, thus allowing for external voices to critique it. This outer-experience gives you enough distance to stare at it in awe, but you're not close enough to be able to protect it. Every time someone asks you whether you're still wanting x, y, and z, you let them take a hammer to your masterpiece and chip away at its beauty. By the time you take another glance at it, the paint's gone, the structure is different, and you're wondering how did you even want it in the first place. There was no work required from you to keep it alive because you weren't the proprietor of the vision in the beginning. But believing in something does the exact opposite. You're required to birth faith within before anyone else sees the fruits of your labor. You're the owner of the vision, not the spectator wishing they had what you created. This faith keeps your task an internal mission that you submit your lifestyle to. You believe in another child. So, you buy them clothes and hang them in their closet. And you create their bathroom and decorate their crib before conception. Your mission is so close to you that the outside world's opinion isn't even relevant. You don't care if you look mad; people thought Noah was out of his mind until they saw the rain. You don't care if you look crazy; Moses didn't even know about the God of Abraham, Isaac, and Jacob. You could care less if other people don't understand. Even Peter tried to rebuke the Messiah for saying someone would murder him one day. Belief, aka your faith, keeps you centered on your goal because the goal is now seen as part of your destiny. It welcomes itself into every area of your life, and you willingly create space for it. No one can walk inside of your heart with a hammer to chip away at your masterpiece. If they even look like they're getting too close, you have the armor to guard it. You treat things differently when you believe in them. You move as if you already possess it because, to be honest, you do.

This is why you have to speak those things that are not as though they are. Let the weak claim themselves to be strong, and the prideful declare themselves as meek. No one else can declare it for you. The words must be formed in your mind, confirmed in your heart, and expelled through your mouth. As an outside source, I can believe in an apple tree all day for you, lest you go and buy the seeds and get to planting; my belief is a waste of time. This is why I refuse to doubt myself. When you believe in something, you work toward it until it manifests itself in the physical realm. Because in the spiritual realm, your belief level has already given it to you. You read that right. Belief gives you the keys to attaining a thing in heavenly places, and your faith is securing it on this side of reality. That's why the birth of my son is as monumental as it is.

For years I wrote to him in a book I used to document the season. I sang to him. I prayed over Camille's womb. I watched sports games as if he was here. I spoke of him in the present tense. Year after year of no physical sign that he'd be a part of our world, I stood firm on preparing a place for him to exist. I knew that if I gave up on him, he'd have no entryway to make it down. I believed that my God was so powerful that Little J's lack of physical presence was about my faith, not whether or not God had the capacity to do it. He made rainbows and tsunamis. He created millions of wildlife species. He made every single human to be different, unique, and complex. Who was I to think sending me a son would be too far outside of his jurisdiction? No, it had to have been my own lack of faith. So I thanked Him for the belief I already had while asking Him to remove my disbelief. I praised Him like it was already done, every single year that we waited. Then in year seven, Camille and I conceived. We were blessed with his life in the year for spiritual completion and rest. God worked for six days and rested on the seventh. God had us work for six years, and we were granted our rest in the seventh. His hand is intentional. Our faith has to match that intention. It has to come into agreement with that focus. It has to wrestle with the angel until our side is touched, and we are blessed with a new covenant. For all righteous desires will be granted unless you throw them by the wayside.

In the early stages, I didn't even need them to check for the gender of our baby because I knew it was our son. All they did by telling us was confirming what I already knew to be true. We had Junior growing and thriving inside my wife's belly, waiting to meet the parents who fought for him to make it over to this world.

Our faith and work-ethic with real estate and the daycares allowed us to send our girls to the top independent schools in the state, and in the midst of that, we met the woman that would deliver our son. Dr. Alexis was a close family friend for over five years and she was officially his godmother. There was never a doubt that she would have that title. She exemplified love for family and a passion for people. She was a perfectionist in her profession. Our older daughters were her daughters' best friends for many years. We even tried to conceive our third child together. Like Jasmine's birth, we had a scheduled C-section for Jemal Jr. on November 20, 2015. Upon arriving at the hospital, Camille was taken to be prepped while I was taken into the backroom with my scrubs to wait for the start of the procedure. As I was in that room, I fell to my knees in prayer and worship, thanking God for seeing us through to this day. For making us wait years for this blessing, for Camille having a smooth pregnancy, for the hands of Dr. Alexis, for Junior's existence, for a safe birth, for the village he had to pray for him, that there was already a place prepared for him; I even thanked Him for the feeling I was about to have once I witnessed the fruits of crazy faith. Uncontrollable tears flowed through the ducts of my eyes as if each tear was another prayer of praise. I was experiencing the hand of God. No one could've forced our son to be born. It didn't matter what treatments were offered; we had to wait on divine timing and trust that it was a delayed matter, not a denied one.

As I watched Camille be the calmest she's ever been in labor, I held her hand, and we awaited the arrival of our only son. I kept my eyes on the birthing team as they worked to get him out of his first home, and realized they were having a bit of a hard time pulling him out based on their conversation. Seconds after realizing this, Dr. Alexis pulled him and responded with a loud and clear, "Whoa!" I was nearly shaking from anticipation. Why was she so shocked? Was he okay? Thoughts began to enter into my mind as I waited to see the very thing I had been sacrificing for, only for the doctor to respond by saying, "He's so long!" By this point, I couldn't take it any longer, and I needed to see my seed. But as perfect as time can become, Dr. Alexis pulled me and asked if I wanted to cut my son's umbilical cord. I stood there awestruck because it was the first time someone said son in reference to one of my children. I knew I was blessed beyond measure. Something that I had prayed for had now become someone that I would love, protect, and guide for the rest of my life. I thought about how much more amazing our lives would soon be with him as I stood there, cutting the cord. Thinking about the toughness of it and how connected he already is to be a King.

After he had been officially removed from his temporary home and laid down, I just remember thinking about being the first person he'd see when he opened his eyes. Camille was doing okay, and her mother was holding her down, so I walked to him and stuck my finger out just to touch his skin. In response, he grabbed my finger with a tightness that felt like a one of a kind bond. Seconds had passed, and he was still holding on as if to say, "I'm here, dad, thank you for not letting go." I heard him. I understood him. I then leaned in to kiss his forehead and to cover him in prayer. The prayer that made me most vulnerable and obedient to God produced fruit more beautiful than I imagined. But just like his older sister, we ran into some issues that night.

After hours had gone by, the staff let us know that they needed to immediately get him to a children's hospital. He hadn't had a bowel movement, and he wasn't taking to feeding, and they needed to see if he was okay before letting us become a family unit. In just a moment, the bliss had disappeared, and we were in action mode. It was the end of November around 1 am during a snowstorm in Chicago when they pulled him away from Camille and began to head to the infant ambulance. Because she underwent surgery, she couldn't go with us, so her mother stepped in while I made sure to trail the ambulance on the way to the hospital. Every mile there, I prayed and said, "God I know you didn't bring us this far only to bring us this far." I was affirming the things that He told me about my son.

I repeated the scriptures that backed up every confirmation He had sent us about Junior's arrival one day. Once we arrived and got inside, they placed him inside an incubator, and I began to speak to him like old times. I read page after page from our documentation book. I talked to him about his family members and how amazing everyone was. I spoke to him about sports and manhood. For his first night in the world, it was the two of us, just like before his birth. It would be God, him, and me talking about what was to come and how we were preparing for his welcome. Before we knew it, five days had passed, and I was balancing staying with him and commuting to be with Camille. Then on his final day, the doctors said nothing was wrong with him; he had taken to eating and nature took its course. Our release day was on the same day—Camille's birthday. It was also the same day that our legacy home had finished being renovated and was ready for us to move in. There were no more confirmations needed to prove that this was the hand of God. I got my wife back, we got our son, and we all were moving into our 18,000 plus square foot home. Our home that'll be passed on for generations to come.

We were able to manifest the fruits of our faithfulness and I was ready to go harder than ever.

From Real Estate To Business Mogul

When my son was born, the first thing I did was buy him a building. We were beyond the point of getting a property for every bill; now, I was stepping into being a businessman. Utilizing real estate as a means to cover our liabilities gave me more freedom to dive into the world of a service-based business. By the time I was in my late thirties, we had owned real estate, daycares, a security company, and a construction company. Needless to say, Camille and I were focused and in a new realm of wealth, opportunity, and enterprise. In the beginning, I stuck with real estate because I had a knack for it. Yes, it was about another stream of income, but if I weren't interested in properties, I wouldn't have been so determined to stick with it. Over time, I was able to transition from being gifted in an area; to managing several businesses, wealth, and a family I had been hoping for since I was a child. This kind of dedication took several hours of me consuming motivational content every week.

I recognized that what went into my temple, whether it was food, music or conversations, dictated what would come out. If all I consumed was content that entertained me instead of empowering me, I wouldn't have the energy to be up by 5:15 am, be a loving husband and father, committed officer (at the time), and an entrepreneur. So I created a routine centered around giving myself what I needed to go hard each and every day. I ate well, trained hard, served others, and consumed content from the likes of Les Brown. Now before YouTube, we would buy CDs of Les Brown's speeches and play them on loop. Every morning, every workout, and even before bed, I'd be filling up my mind with Les.

Some of my favorite quotes from him include:
"If you want to grow and develop yourself, embrace failure. If you want to become the best at

what you do, you've got to be willing to fail again and again. And then finally, one day, you can fail your way to greatness."

"Your dream was given to you. If someone else can't see it for you, that's fine, it was given to you and not them. It's your dream. Hold it. Nourish it. Cultivate it!"

"You are the only real obstacle in your path to a fulfilling life."

"When life knocks you down, try to land on your back. Because if you can look up, you can get up."

For years I was an avid consumer of Les Brown before I was introduced to another motivational speaker. Then YouTube popped up, and after some years, I began to exchange my CDs for video links. Evolving with the times, I maintained my original routine, but I was happy to see I didn't need to have access to a CD player anymore. That was until I listened to a round of videos on autoplay when a compilation mix came on. I wasn't sure what it was, but it started with Les Brown, so I didn't question the title. But after minutes, I heard this loudmouth man screaming about hard-work, dedication, and commitment. I won't lie; I was offended. I remember thinking, "Who is this dude interrupting Les?!" As a dedicated listener, I had half a mind to change the video and go back to what I was used to. That was until I started listening to what this man was yelling. Phrases like, "If you want to succeed as bad as you want to breathe..." and "Don't think you're going to get success on a discount..." went off through my eardrums and struck fire into my soul. For a moment, I felt like I was betraying Les as I was being motivated by someone that referred to themselves as the HipHop Preacher. I didn't know who this man was, where he had come from, or why his words were striking gold, but I knew that I needed to listen to him just as much, if not more than Les.

It was around 2012 when I started listening to Eric Thomas. Within days his videos became an integral part of my routine. When I'd wake up, I'd always send a verse to my friends and family, but now I was sending them a scripture with a link. By the time I listened to Eric, it felt like he had already pushed out hundreds of videos. It wasn't the same as consuming Les's content because eventually, there'd be an end. But with E, I could let his videos play all day every day without hitting the ceiling. That was huge for me because although it was still motivation, I was getting different messages. After all, he covered various topics. It wasn't any of that "ra ra ra go hard" mess. He had real gems to share in his content. I could tell he was living the lifestyle he was preaching about online. Hustle always recognizes hustle, and there was no way he would have been able to bring that kind of energy into his videos had it not been real to him. For years I consumed his content before they launched their first conference in 2014. I didn't even know about it until Camille told me. Initially, I was amped because I figured she'd want to come with me. To my surprise, she thought I should go with Vontrell, my first son.

Now I know you just read that and became confused, so here's the story of our relationship. In 2010, Camille and I brought Vontrell into our lives to live with us. Growing up, I had a favorite uncle named Lester, who was all about athletics and health. Naturally, he took me underneath his wing because of my desire to play pro-football. He'd take me for 4 am runs, go through various drills, and advise on any matter I brought to him. It's wild because once I was older, I realized that uncle Lester used to buy, renovate, and flip older-historic properties too. With that said, you can see how much of an influence this specific uncle was on me.

Well, uncle Lester had a daughter who then had a son named Vontrell. I didn't know the full depths of the relationship, but I was aware that his father wasn't present in his life at the time. Over a length of time, my uncle started to become sickly. On a holiday that I can't remember, he called his daughter to inform her that he was terminally ill and battling cancer. The report that the doctor gave him was sure of a soon death. As any child would be, she was broken down by this news, so broken though that she had a massive heart attack immediately after talking to her father. Vontrell and his younger brother were witnesses to her falling out, but by the time special care reached their home, she had already passed on. In a moment, he learned of his grandfather's illness and lost his mother. Within the week, they had to prepare for his mother's funeral, and the morning of the ceremony, his grandfather passed on while getting ready for the service. A broken heart had taken two people out of two children's lives.

For Vontrell specifically, he was immediately placed in a rough situation. His father lived in Florida, and the only other next to kin that was alive was his great-grandmother. Trying to honor the parental order, Vontrell then moved out to Florida to live with a man he never had a relationship with. It's safe to say that it wasn't an ideal circumstance, and Vontrell would soon move back and in with his great grandmother. My cousin Tyra began to whisper to me how Vontrell needed some male guidance and help with his athletics. I wasn't immediately led to bring him into my home. I was a father of two young girls, and their safety was my number one focus. I decided to do for him the things that my uncle Lester did for me. Before we knew it, I was picking him up from practice, taking him to training sessions at 4 am, going for jogs, discussing his studies, and everything else he needed.

This lasted for a period of time until Father's Day came, and Vontrell was riding around with me. I asked him whether or not he had reached out to his biological father, and he told me that he hadn't. In my ignorance of the depth of their strained relationship, I pushed him to call and wish his dad a happy father's day. I gave him my phone and watched him dial the numbers and watch it ring until his pops eventually answered. Picking up the phone with an attitude, he asked who was calling him. Vontrell proceeded to tell him who it was and that he was calling to wish him a happy father's day. I kid you not; his dad immediately responded by saying, "Man didn't I tell you to leave me alone? You've got your life out there, and I've got mine. Leave me the f alone." before he hung up the line. Vontrell was broken-hearted all over again and began to cry out in anger, telling me how he knew his dad didn't want anything to do with him. And although it was a heart wrenching moment to experience, I needed to see just how broken their relationship was. I hugged him and let him know that he didn't have to worry about that ever again; I had him. From that day forward, I started having him spend the night, every single night, at our home.

Camille was looking at me, trying to figure out what I was doing, bringing a fifteen-year-old into our house without talking to her about it at length. I knew that I didn't have the option to not be an earthly covering for Vontrell, though. I had an obligation to protect the harmony we created in our family, but I also felt the need to be a father figure for Vontrell. Time passed on, and Vontrell had gotten so comfortable with us and we with him; that he called Camille "mom" and eventually referred to me as "dad." I had no idea that the son I had been praying for would first appear as a fifteen -year-old teenager that stood 6'3 at nearly 250 lbs. Being frank, a village helped raise this young man. It was an honor to witness him change his last name to King. I truly believe God gave us a biological son because He allowed us to take care of someone else's. We did it without strife, without judgment, and without expectation of any materialistic return.

This is why Camille wanted Vontrell to go with me instead.. I won't hold you, though, once I found out that the conference was in Hartford, Connecticut, and my wife wasn't going with me, it didn't sound too exciting. I figured that I wouldn't miss out on anything as long as I kept consuming the content. Camille wasn't having that, though. She convinced me that we should finally go, and it ended up being one of the most extraordinary life-changing experiences I've ever had.

By 2014 my net worth was somewhere around eleven million, if not a little more. I didn't want to attend the conference to learn how to make more money; I knew that I needed some fuel to keep sustaining what I was doing for my family. Since I intended to get a life-changing experience, I bought Vontrell and I VIP tickets, we flew first class, and we stayed in the best hotel suite. If we were coming out, we were coming out strong. I'm a firm believer in never undercutting yourself because you think your comfort isn't as important as the core event. If you have the means to do it, then ensure your entire experience matches the energy of the conference you're attending. That itself will make all the difference.

After landing at the airport and getting unpacked in our hotel, we were excited to see what Eric Thomas and Associates was about to present. Mind you; this was the second personal development conference I ever attended. So when we walked up for registration, I was blown away. I can remember telling myself that this was on a whole new level from what I experienced before. It was like we were surrounded by kindred spirits, people full of energy, and ready to attack the day. You didn't hear, "Man it's too early," "I wish I were home," or "I hope this goes by fast." Now, I have some amazing friends in Chicago, but this kind of hype was different. My batteries were getting recharged, and I didn't even know they needed to be. Within minutes I knew I would be attending every conference they advertised and bringing new people with me. My family needed to experience how refreshing it was to be around people excited about life and what was to come. There was a gap in the circle that I had, and I knew the conference was going to present a well-needed blessing.

Throughout the stages of my life, I spent my time in prayer asking for blessings. I asked for a career, a house to pass down to my legacy, a family to care for, good health, the ability to make an impact —and I received it all. In my thirties, my prayers began to shift from more blessings to changing my circle of friends and influence. We have often heard that iron sharpens iron, and I knew the value I could bring to a friendship. It was time. I could not only pour into people, but I also needed to get poured back into. I was praying for men I could build with and talk about my family with. I had access to people who talked about the past, and I met people whose focus was the future. People that knew the good ole days were ahead of them, not behind.

Time went on during the event and I still remember this pivotal moment in my 9 to 5 millionaire journey. It was in the middle of the VIP dinner after the Greatness is Upon You Conference, and I got to meet CJ, who introduced himself to me and asked where I was from, what I did for a living and how I heard about Eric Thomas. Next thing I know, Eric Thomas walks up to our table and we begin to talk at length. It felt like I was talking to a friend from ten years ago, not someone that I was meeting for the first time. Of course, he asked me how we learned about the conference, and I let him know Camille was the one that encouraged us to get here. When he asked where she was, and I let him know she was holding down the fort at home, he offered for us to make a video together to say hey. CJ got the phone and a resounding, "What up, what up, what up" came from the lungs of Eric. It's amazing how we always get these tiny snippets of what life will be like in the future based on things that happen during our present day. At the moment, it was just a video for Camille, but years later, we're in hundreds of videos together. Once we finished recording, I met Karl, Dede, and more members of the ETA squad.

To think, while I was praying for God to change my circle of influence, I never would have thought He would bring the #1 influencer in the world into my circle. Exceedingly, abundantly, above all that we could ask or think is real. All we need to do is remain obedient and focused; He'll bring every answer to every gap we have. The best part about being connected to the team was knowing that wasn't even my angle. I didn't need a handout or an opportunity. I was focused on getting the information I needed to take back home.

I value exposure to the utmost. You can't put a price tag on the exposure Vontrell and I received in Hartford. Especially knowing how his life would pan out. He not only thrived on the collegiate level, but became a successful collegiate coach by the time he was twenty-five. A feat that thirty-year-old men would envy. Every single day he gets to pour back into young men that were just like him. He has become to them what I was for him, all because I was able to invest in his life. That's the level of impact that comes with investing into the lives of others. So when Camille convinced us that we should go to the conference; I knew we just needed to be in the building. As soon as we concluded our stay and wrapped every workshop, VIP dinner and lecture, Vontrell and I headed back to Chicago with new eyes and perspectives.

I can do all things through Christ who strengthens me

PHILIPPIANS 4:13

Chapter 15

9TH MILE MENTALITY

Training for a marathon as a previous football player wasn't an easy feat. Football is a sport that requires speed, power and explosiveness, and the ability to start and stop and pivot quickly. As you can imagine, I didn't need any of these skills for running twenty plus miles. The muscle memory my body had acquired for one sport, didn't quickly transfer over for the new one. At 6'3 and 222 lbs, I spent four months training for my first long-distance race, which remarkably enough happened to be a marathon. I knew I wanted to do it because I could tell my body and mind needed a shock. For me, that's always easiest by changing up my new training regimen. For you, it could be picking up a new language, a new dance, a 1000 piece puzzle, or whatever. But I find it satisfying to remind my body that it can always get better, stronger, and in this case, more enduring.

I don't care what age I am or what I'm used to, if there's a healthy way I can put my body through a test; I'm taking it. That's why a marathon sounded so appealing. I had never run for that amount of time before, neither had I taken on that form of training. Little did I know how different the actual competition was compared to sports like football, volleyball and tennis. It's for this revelation that I'll never forget my first race. To start the race, they shot off the gun, and we all went running. You're surrounded by what feels like thousands of people with the same goal in mind: endure until the end. Unlike sports like basketball, these people weren't my competition. We weren't divided up by teams, but rather by how fast our times were. I had to quickly learn that this kind of competition is about keeping pace and going against time itself, not the person to my left, right, front, or behind. It's you and time; that's it. It doesn't matter how strong someone looks on the first three miles, not even the first five. The moment you decide to run their pace and not the speed you established via training, you start to run their race instead of your own. At first, I disliked not having a physical competitor. But the more I ran, the more I became anchored in the idea of time because of my marker of success. Eventually, I learned that marathons are carbon copies of our life cycles. We're not competing against our neighbors or co-workers, our only race is against time. As humans, we only have a designated amount of time in this world. This explains why Ecclesiastes 9:11 says, "The race is not given to the swift nor the strong but he who endures until the end." That's the ninth-mile mentality. No matter where I compete, there's something about the ninth mile that exposes everything about a runner.

They might've looked like the most efficient athlete you've ever seen, but as soon as they hit mile number nine, their breathing falls apart, their legs begin to give way, and their self-talk begins to turn sour. The ninth mile is when you see people you started with fall off, and you have to decide whether you'll slow down or speed up to meet people that are running your pace. Once I got this, I fell in love with marathons. The entire challenge is based on how consistent you can be. When others pass you or slow down, can you stay loyal to the pace you've spent weeks, sometimes months, training for? That's why the only equipment you need is a watch. It's showing you whether or not you understand time, consistency, and sticking with your plan for over twenty miles. There's no need to try and push yourself even harder because running twenty plus miles is already hard work. Letting your emotions make you outrun your pace in miles two and three could be detrimental to miles four and five. Instead of looking like a runner, you'll start moving like a swimmer cutting through the air, losing your efficiency, pace, and over course, time advantage. One decision to try and outdo yourself when you weren't ready will make you waiver for the upcoming distances. So now you're losing time because you wavered in your consistency. That's the scary part about life. No matter how big a pill it is to swallow, you slowing down doesn't slow down time itself. Time exists and continues, no matter what you're doing. It isn't predicated on your good or bad decisions. It isn't even predicated on your mere existence. Seconds will continue to flow, whether or not you're using it wisely or not. Doing what you need to do in the immediate influences your future! Keeping pace for the first thirteen miles sets the tone for your second half.

I pray that you're getting this because it's a life truth. Teach this to your mentees and children. Make this a life practice for yourself. Whatever you have to do, learn this as fast as you can, because time won't slow down for you to master this either.

Although marathons are individual-based events, you can always train and compete with a group of people. It gives you a team that you're held accountable to and adds another layer of excitement. A key factor for who you bring on to your team is pace. Do these people all run the same pace as you? Are they training on their own for this pace? Do you think they'd try to break pace by speeding up too early or slowing down? Do you have the same goal in mind and timeline? Being able to answer these questions confidently lets you know who your team members should be, and I'm not just talking about running a marathon; I mean in life. Finding these people as you're going through your run, aka your life's journey, gives you well-needed motivation. They'll inspire you to go even harder in training so you can be who they need on race day. In case you need a reminder, everything you do behind doors will always show itself in the light, and I'm sure you don't want to be the person that lets the team down.

Without subjecting your body to intense training and recovery, there's no way you'll be ready for a marathon. Taking your mental, physical, and even spiritual work lightly will expose itself once you hit mile number nine, and your team members will have to decide whether to forsake themselves or stay committed to their goal. Like a relay, minus the different positions, any misstep could disqualify you from the race itself or hitting your target. It's the same with your life. Several factors could disqualify you from passing down generational wealth. But don't let this discourage you, let it put a fire underneath you! Your past might've slowed you down, but you can now redirect your energy and start a new race. You might not be able to get it all done in three years, but that shouldn't stop you from aiming for the next ten or twenty.

It's because of this level of consistency, account- ability, and mastery that I love my brotherhood with ETA. Working with a team that doesn't slow down has shown me how important it is to run with people with marathon mindsets. Every one of them appreciates the time they have, which is huge because most people don't. The masses inherently believe they have more time than they do. They might not explicitly say this, but their actions speak volumes over their words. The lack of reading, exercising, studying, and eating as healthy as possible shows where their beliefs lay. One thing I've never had to worry about with CJ, Eric, Karl, and Josh is how they view time. We understand that our lives are only the totality of how we use our time. I need you to get this. Your present is evidence of how you used your time in the past. Your future is the total of how you're us- ing your time now. Make decisions based on this information, and I can promise that your life will begin to shift in ways you deemed impossible. The man that respects time is the man that finds favor in it. It's telling God that you recognize your life is but a vapor, so you're going to do all you can to honor the milliseconds that you're alive on this earth. I saw this in the men at ETA and recognized it within myself. Our ability to accept time goes back to having faith in tomorrow despite what we see today. All of us rely on faith and not just sight. That's how all of this took off in the first place. A group of men came together that were all walking in their power individually, so by the time I got into the picture, elevation was a must. I know for a fact that I'm running my ninth mile with ETA. Although every man can fall off, I trust that each of us will uphold our commitment because iron sharpens iron. There's too much fruit to prove every man is who he says he is.

You should have this same level of confidence and trust in your team. Whether it's your mentors, peers that turn family, or your staff, can you trust that they'll do all that they can to remain loyal to the vision you all dreamed up? Will they do all they can to not only build their legacies but to help you build yours? Will you do all you can to build your foundation, so they have something to build on? Running with godly men has fine-tuned my gifts in leadership and communication. It's enhanced my ability to be a strong covering for my wife. It's allowed me to be an even better father. By remaining faithful day in and out, I'm keeping the pace that I set years ago when I said

I wanted to be a millionaire. By running with this group of upstanding men, I've even learned how to be a well-rounded employer, recognizing that we all have different personality traits and how we can best utilize what we naturally do. CJ isn't lying when he says you can't compartmentalize greatness. You're going to go all-in, or you're going to suffer the consequences of being imbalanced. A great team helps you assess how you're doing holistically in the race, not just if you're doing well in business.

It still wows me how we are all connected. I was thirty-six when I attended the first ETA conference, and I was forty when we all became a unit. Kid you not, at one of the conferences, CJ and I exchanged contact information with the intentions of being in touch. Being on the outside, I could see how much work CJ had to do, so I never wanted to be the person who bothered him. Instead of calling, we'd just see each other from conference to conference and hit a, "Man, we got to stay in touch." I'm sure both of us had full intentions of contacting the other, but it never happened. Then, after four years, I got a call from CJ at 7 pm while I was in the kitchen with Camille. I was shocked, surprised, bewildered—whatever you want to call it. I immediately assumed it must've been a butt-dial, but I answered anyway. So when CJ said, "What's up, Jemal!" I looked at Camille in disbelief. Getting that call on that day was the most unexpected blessing, but I still assumed that he was just making calls to loyal fans, and I was next up on the list. As we began to speak, we both acknowledged how cool the other was. I wasn't fanning out, but I wondered why this man with 30,000 things to do was taking out the time to call me, a conference attendee, at 7 pm. After a few minutes of chopping it up, we hung up, and we went about our evenings. I figured that it was nothing more than the team wanting to check-in on their community members, but regardless, I was grateful.

Time passed by and, just as random as the first; I got another call from CJ. At this point, I thought their customer service skills were on a thousand. I wasn't trying to be a part of the team, nor did I attempt to interfere with their schedules. All I wanted to do was attend their conferences to bring that energy back to my family. There wasn't one piece of me that was trying to be down with the squad. Looking back, I'm sure that's what made our friendship so easy. This time CJ called me to let me know that Eric had a corporate gig in Chicago and wanted to invite me out to the Cheesecake Factory for dinner. Again, I was caught off guard in the best way possible. I let him know that Camille and I would be there. At arrival, I still had no idea what they saw in me that made them want to sit down. I've always been humble, so I definitely valued the invitation to get to know them better. At the time, they had no idea of the companies that we created. All they knew was I was an officer that owned some real estate on the side. They had no idea I was a multi-millionaire that was a cop on the side. It was a fantastic experience, though. My wife got to meet CJ's wife, Candis, and Eric's wife Dede and they talked the entire time. I got to kick it with CJ and Eric, and they asked me about my life story. At first, I gave the real estate and officer spill. That was until CJ asked Camille what she did for a living, and we let them know we owned daycare centers too. As you can imagine, this was a huge surprise. Up until that point, I had painted a picture that I was a man living a slightly above average life. We dived into the details of that business until I saw two of my officers outside, and I let the table know they were two of my guys. Of course, they asked for what venture, and I realized I never told them about the security company I own with my brother Tommie. In the matter of an hour, I had gone from Jemal, the cop to Jemal, the businessman who still worked a 9 to 5. CJ was astonished, to say the least, and asked me how in the heck I was able to do all this. This was one of the first times I was able to talk about all the work Camille and I had been doing for years. It was a great dinner, to say the least. It wasn't even a few days later when CJ called me up to invite me to Jersey with the team for Eric and CJ to speak. To be honest, I still thought this was some elite fandom experience. Obviously, I went, because who'd turn that down? Funny enough, this would be the trip that catapulted me into the speaking realm, and I didn't even have a slideshow prepared.

We got to the session where CJ was the speaker, and he killed it. It was great to sit in the crowd and take notes on the gems that he dropped.

Once Q&A started up, I wasn't thinking about my time to shine. I was an attendee in my eyes, not a resource for the people. CJ, however, saw differently. A couple of people started to ask him about real estate, and he immediately deferred to me. He let them know he only had real estate in the house he laid his head at night, and if they wanted to know about the industry, they needed to come to talk to me. Immediately CJ handed me a microphone, and I began to answer their questions. It was unnatural, it felt uncomfortable, and I was in shock. According to CJ, I was operating in my gift. So much so, he pulled out his phone and recorded my responses to their real estate questions. Because I spent over a decade in the field, it was easy to give them advice. I've invested since my early twenties. There would be very little that could throw me off when talking about properties. At the end of the Q&A, a huge line formed in front of me to ask me more questions. Although I wasn't expecting this to happen, all the training I've done prepared me to serve them effectively. Once the lines cleared, and CJ and I got a moment to talk, he let me know that they were launching a new tour called Take Control, and he'd love for me to sit on a panel discussing real estate. They wanted to give people practical advice on how they could start being lenders and not borrowers. Because of my love for serving people, I agreed.

It was amazing to experience this side of the conference. For years I was only an attendee. I couldn't have imagined the amount of preparation that went into setting up a tour, traveling, studying and everything that came along with it.Being on the other side for the first time was mind blowing. There's something special about going from one city to another and providing the same, yet customized experience. The crowd in New York was different from the ones in Texas, and Texas was different from Georgia. Speaking of which, Atlanta was the night that put the cherry on top of my speaking career. Just like every other stop, I was able to sit on a panel with Eric, C.J, and Josh and give out information that was changing hundreds to thousands of people's lives. They were simple responses for the most part, but the content was so practical that everyone should've left that conference and made a change in their lives. For the most part, things did remain in this order until; I was asked a question that hit me in my soul. I'd be lying if I said I remember exactly what the question was, but all I know was that I felt a burst of lightning from the crown of my head to the soles of my feet. It didn't help that this was the first conference Camille was able to attend with me on the panel. Between getting asked a question that ignited my fire and seeing my wife in the crowd, I stood up and began to give a passionate speech about perseverance, faith, and pressing forward. I spoke every word with confidence, and I spoke with authority. I remember feeling like the words coming out of my mouth weren't my own; instead, words that every soul in those seats needed to hear. By the time I sat down, I had come back to myself, and CJ and Eric leaned over to quietly whisper,

"Welcome to your new life." That's when I finally started to see what God had planned for this union and that's also when C.J dubbed me the "9 to 5 Millionaire."

Finally Reaching Retirement

It was no surprise that God had already started establishing the second half of my life when I reached my point of retirement. I had given the Chicago Police Department twenty years of my life, twenty loyal and productive years at that. I didn't allow being a millionaire to make me lazy or dead weight on the job. I did what was needed, and I did it well. People always ask why I still worked a 9 to 5 into my early forties, even though I didn't need to. What they don't understand is that I didn't start planning for retirement in my thirties. I started planning for retirement as soon as I was hired. I knew that I only intended to give the force ten or twenty years of my life, nothing more. This is still an early retirement because more people are lucky if they retire after thirty years. My parents are the ones that counseled me into working for twenty instead of ten. They taught me that I'd still be a young man in my forties, and I'd get all the benefits of retirement rather than just leaving the job. Now, telling someone in their twenties that they'd still be a young man at forty-one sounds like a joke. It's crazy being on the other side of it because I feel exactly how my parents promised; young and full of life. I'm sure my family and I would've been fine without the extra ten-year commitment, but if time is going to pass by regardless, then I might as well get as many benefits from my labor as possible. Being an officer wasn't stopping me from living out my dreams. I worked a job; I didn't let it work me. Maintaining this mentality every year for twenty years allowed me to prepare for retirement when I stepped foot on the job. I knew I would be retired early, and I trusted I'd do what I needed to make that a reality. The truth is, when you believe in something, you prepare for that thing to manifest itself.

Answering that question is going to help you make decisions that match your desired outcome. I knew that retiring from the force didn't mean I was done working for the rest of my life. It just meant that I was done clocking into someone else's establishment. I was preparing myself to give them twenty good years, while also making each year great for myself. As you remember, I don't believe in the age-old retirement philosophy that says, give them your best thirty to forty years of your life, and enjoy your worst ten. No. I believe in delivering what's needed, but ultimately pouring the most into my household. Had I waited to make legacy-based moves until I retired, I wouldn't even be writing this book. Our children wouldn't be in the positions they are, nor would they have access to the educational and athletic resources they have. We might not even have three children. My wife would be working for a company she potentially hates. Our relationship would have to fight the strain of stress. I probably wouldn't have retired by forty-one.

All in all, everything about my life would've never existed, or it would've been altered. You would've never known my name was Jemal King. I wouldn't have been able to help flip properties for my older sister or start a security company with my brother. Camille and I wouldn't have been able to cut a retirement check for my mother from the daycare. Nor would my brother and I pay out a check to my father from the security company. Without the daycares, we wouldn't have been able to create free childcare opportunities for friends and family, allowing them to invest their money elsewhere.

Because of our ability to understand vehicles and destinations, we've been able to do all things for our children. There isn't a "no" we give them that correlates to financial strain. There's nothing we aren't able to do for our kids. With their future tuition getting paid to starting a company for them right now and getting them their first investment property. From private tennis lessons to private schooling, the blessing is that we set them up in conditions that'll make it extremely hard for them to fail. They're in the position they're in today because of what Camille and I did yesterday. We know it's our job to give them foundations they can build empires on. It took God blessing our consistency and wisdom. I've told you several times throughout this book that there's nothing insanely special about me other than my ability to do what I say. Can't you taste how your life would be if you did the same? Can't you smell it, feel it, and see it? Can't you hear what your great-grandchildren will say about your obedience if you start now? You don't have to do something as major as purchasing your first property, but you could do something as minimal as walking for twenty minutes a day. You don't have to make a million in 365 days, but you could bring in an extra $20,000 from an online sales venture. You just need to figure out what you want your life to look like in the next ten years, and stick to your vision.

That's all I did; I set-up my life by the decades. Every birthday between, although important, isn't what I use to measure if I've been loyal to my word. A year isn't a long enough time to test how faithful I've been, but ten? Ten years is absolutely enough time to reflect, assess, and pivot. Every decade you have to re-envision your life. You have to keep assessing your previous visions because each season brings a new exposure level. You don't want to have the same vision at forty that you had at twenty or thirty. Had I not gone back to look at what twenty-year-old me said when I turned thirty, I would've been a thirty-year-old with the mind and dreams of a young adult. Using the wisdom I gained over that decade helped me re-assess and build on top of my foundation. This is why I feel so blessed to be in my forties. Twenty-year-old Jemal dreamed. Thirty-year-old Jemal executed. Forty-year-old me can move mountains now. That's not limited to my life story; it's able to exist in yours too. One key you'll need to do this is to shift from being a consumer to being a producer. By focusing on what you're putting out into the world rather than what the world is giving you, you'll increase in wisdom, finances and wellness. Producers make decisions that influence everyone else that's sitting around, waiting to be entertained and directed. We focus on being co-creators on this earth, even in our 9 to 5s, while consumers concentrate on working a job that dictates their every second. When you think like this, you'll use your job as your fuel in the early stages. Your job is your business's first investor; treat it as such. See yourself as the mogul you are. See your work as impactful because it will be. If you continue to move by what's in front of you, you'll never reap a real harvest. Your eyes will lie to you; you know the verse, walk by faith and not by sight. The real value in life lies in the things you cannot see. One thing my thirties taught me was things don't just happen. They have to be seen, planned, and executed. At a 9 to 5, people tell you what to do, when to do it, and how to do it. They can't, and they won't tell you how to make your dreams come true. That's on you to do. You can't think of something amazing and just sit on it anymore. If you don't do it, then it won't get done. Your emotions don't matter when it comes to the desire of your life. So what you don't feel like walking for twenty minutes today. Are you physically capable of doing it, and are you safe? If the answer is yes to both of those questions, then get up and get it done. That's why the Word says to let your yes be yes, and your no be no. You don't need to do anything else except for honoring the covenants you make with your mouth. Take care of yourself so you can be faithful to your life's work, even if you don't know it yet. And in everything, give it your all. You will only get out what you put in.

Success Is In My DNA

Over time I've learned that I come from a family of producers. From my late uncle, who flipped properties to my father who ranked to sergeant, it is a blessing to be the seed of men who did what they said they were going to do. On top of that, we have a close-knit family. We often host a family reunion to make sure relationships are still being fostered, and kinship isn't being lost. One year was special, though. The family reunion committee had been working to build our family tree. They had gone through name after name in a census until they found our great-great-great grandfather. With a little more research, they were able to find his will through the archives. As a Black man, this is huge. Slave owners messed up so many of our last names by changing them and not documenting marriages and misspelling names that it's hard to trace where your people are from. Unless your family used the Bible method that wrote down who such and such married, who divorced, who died, and who was born, and made sure it got passed down through generations, it's hard to keep up with the lives of our forefathers. So finding our great-great-great grandfather Washington Winston and learning he even had a will, was beyond us. I couldn't wait to get my hands on it, and I'm glad I did. The will was written in 1878, only thirteen years after the

13th Amendment, and man was it insightful. Our patriarch on my mother's side had left each of his five kids five acres, and his wife twenty acres of land, a house, wagons, mules, and livestock. Proverbs 13:22 rang through my mind as I held his will in my hand. "A blessed man will leave an inheritance to his children's children..." Despite being born in a time where human enslavement was overtly supported, he found ways to leave an inheritance for his family. We aren't sure what happened to this land, or if the state even upheld his will, but to see how selfless he was brought a flood of emotions to me. This man could have easily let the trauma he experienced and the trauma his parents endured make him give up. To be frank, he could've done that, and the world would have had to understand. To date, there's nothing like the traumas endured by survivors of the Transatlantic slave-trade. But he didn't. He wanted to ensure his wife and his children could go on and live even after his passing. The part that struck gold for me was that he used real estate to do it. This moment confirmed success being a generational blessing. One man decided to give all he had, and we've been reaping the benefits ever since. No, not in money. No, not in real estate. But in work-ethic, mentality, and drive. I learned that success flowed through my DNA, and I couldn't contain the tears. As my pastor John F. Hannah from New Life Covenant in Chicago always says, "One man's obedience is connected to so many other people's destiny." It was quick reminder that our history didn't start, nor did it stop with slavery. Our DNA had survived every single world war, famine, depression, recession, slave order, genocide, and natural disaster that hit our people. We were still alive, breathing. We were still reproducing seeds despite what the world had thrown at us. I was reminded that we were kings and queens. Our minds were and still are brilliant. Even as I sit here writing this, I'm full of emotions and hope for you. All it took was one man to start a legacy in our family, a man whose name we didn't even know. I'm asking you to start the success gene for your lineage.

Visualize your great-great-great-grandchildren living life on the left side of the menu. Faith is all you need to build a legacy. The things you will rely on your faith to accomplish will be immeasurable. Using faith is like planting a forest. Planting one seed establishes so much. And just because you don't see the first tree growing, doesn't mean something isn't taking place under the ground. Once you let your roots take hold and shoot through the soil to become a strong tower, you'll begin to multiply over and over again. Before you know it, the fruits of your labor have conceived an entire forest. Let the image in your mind drive you and keep you determined to plant. Faith is the seed; the image is the water. Let that image become so real that you can't ignore it. The way I couldn't ignore my son before his entrance into this world, you've got to know that your dream is as real as my unborn son was to me. It has to be more real than anything you can see right now because the world is nothing more than the evidence of someone's imagination.

Chapter 16

THE NEW BLUE COLLAR

So that's my recipe for success. By tailoring my vision to be larger than life, training my mind to go after challenges, applying wisdom to the exposure I received, honing in on being an efficient decision-maker, and outlining what legacy meant for me, I was able to become the 9 to 5 Millionaire. There is no magic sauce or shortcut to sustainable wealth. For nearly twenty years, I've been able to not only make money, but keep it and use it to change the lives of those I haven't even met. That's wealth. My prayer is that you go out and do the same. I have no desire to get you hype if you're not going to do the work. My final call to action is to take immediate action as soon as you close this book. For additional clarity I've listed some step-by-step directions.

#1 - Assess your current situation. Write down what can stay the same, what needs to grow, and what needs to go.

#2 - Assess your character. Are you the kind of person that takes responsibility for yourself and those around you?

#3 - Write down your values and assess if they match your actions.

#4a - Establish decade long personal, financial, and physical goals. This is where you take the time to outline your destination and evaluate your vision. For efficiency, break your decade goal down into bite-size year and ninety-day goals. It should look like an upside triangle. This is where you dream again!

#4b - Have the unwavering faith that what you've set for your life will come to pass. Think of transitioning from wanting to possessing your goal.

#5 - Analyze the vehicles you have access to. Can they get you to your destination? What sources of income do you already have or can get quick access to?

#6 - Make a plan for your vehicles. Figure out how your current vehicle can move you closer to your destination, and what other vehicles you might use. Don't forget, your vehicles are here for you to use, never let them use you!

#7 - Look into your network and see who might help you or who you can invest in. This includes resources. For example, the Make Real Estate Real course would be an example of a resource you could use to make real estate a viable vehicle for you. It has definitely worked for me.

#8- Get exposed at all costs! Treat exposure like the new currency! Remember that your level of exposure will determine your level of success!

#9 - Self-assess your progress every quarter, aka ninety days. Make adjustments based on where you've succeeded and where you've failed. I recommend keeping a journal so you can see your progress over time. Remember you are doing this for the future you!

I promise it's not deeper than this. Anytime you learn from anyone, including me, you should always take the core of our messages and make it applicable to yourself. One reason people don't get results is that they overcomplicate the process; thus, they don't make any moves. Sadly, I know some of you will fall into this category too. I know this to be true because there are people that have watched me make millions for nearly twenty years that still don't invest in themselves or think they can do it too.

On the other hand, some people have talked to me for twenty minutes that immediately changed their legacies. I can't count how many times I've told you there's nothing special about me. The information I hold is information that can be widely used. So yes, you just read an entire book about my story, but who cares. The greater picture is to make it yours! This book's purpose was to make you see what's possible for your life, not to marvel at mine.

I'm a Black man from Chicago, raised by blue-collar parents, and worked a blue-collar job too. I wasn't given an inheritance of financial wealth. Like you, I've had to build everything that I have for myself. As people, we're responsible for our outcomes. Reading books won't be enough to change your life. The doctor doesn't heal the patient; the patient heals themself by putting the doctor's orders into action. Decide now whether or not you're going to use the gems you've been given. For those of you who have been fighting but still don't see the fruits of your labor, please don't give up on me. The issue might not be your will nor your determination, but rather your vehicle. Evaluate how far you can go with the job you have (i.e., what's the max salary you could make) and see how you need to pivot. You're dreaming the right dream, I promise. Do not, I repeat, do not give up your dream or your vision because things haven't unfolded for you yet. You're closer than you think. Do you remember my pastor John Hannah's quote about the connection of one man's obedience being the connection to so many other people's destiny? Who's counting on you to do what you are supposed to do so they can become who they're supposed to? This is why I tell people about real estate so often. I know it's one of the few vehicles that couldn't reach a cap, and if it can, I'm nowhere near it.

My greatest hope is that you'll be a part of the generation that redefines what it means to be blue-collar. Even with the global turmoil that we're experiencing, I believe that things will work out for our good. Choose life on this day by choosing to shift how you perceive yourself and challenges. With this change, you'll always be more than a conqueror and never forget that your future is counting on you!

And if I could leave you with any quote of mine, I'll leave you with this. If your dreams don't require you to have crazy faith, then you need to dream bigger!

Signed,

Jemal King

9 to 5 millionaire

JEMAL KING™